T0191049

WRITTEN
IN THE
STARS

Also by Kate Rose

You Only Fall in Love Three Times:
The Secret Search for Our Twin Flame

WRITTEN
IN THE
STARS

The Astrology of SOULMATE,
KARMIC, and TWIN FLAME
Relationships

KATE ROSE

New World Library
Novato, California

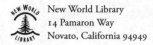 New World Library
14 Pamaron Way
Novato, California 94949

Copyright © 2024 by Kate Rose

All rights reserved. This book may not be reproduced in whole or in part, stored in a retrieval system, or transmitted in any form or by any means — electronic, mechanical, or other — without written permission from the publisher, except by a reviewer, who may quote brief passages in a review.

The material in this book is intended for education. It is not meant to take the place of diagnosis and treatment by a qualified medical practitioner or therapist. No expressed or implied guarantee of the effects of the use of the recommendations can be given or liability taken.

Text design by Tona Pearce Myers

Library of Congress Cataloging-in-Publication Data

Title: Written in the stars : the astrology of soulmate, karmic, and twin flame relationships / Kate Rose.
Description: Novato, California : New World Library, [2024] | Summary: "An astrological guide to relationships that shows readers how to find lasting love and avoid unfulfilling patterns that lead to heartbreak. Includes birth charts, and detailed discussions of the ways that lesser-known astrological factors can affect the success of relationships"-- Provided by publisher.
Identifiers: LCCN 2024023028 (print) | LCCN 2024023029 (ebook) | ISBN 9781608689156 (paperback) | ISBN 9781608689163 (epub)
Subjects: LCSH: Astrology. | Love--Miscellanea. | Mate selection--Miscellanea. | Interpersonal relations--Miscellanea.
Classification: LCC BF1729.L6 R67 2024 (print) | LCC BF1729.L6 (ebook) | DDC 133.5--dc23/eng/20240701
LC record available at https://lccn.loc.gov/2024023028
LC ebook record available at https://lccn.loc.gov/2024023029

First printing, September 2024
ISBN 978-1-60868-915-6
Ebook ISBN 978-1-60868-916-3
Printed in Canada

New World Library is committed to protecting our natural environment. This book is made of material from well-managed FSC®-certified forests and other controlled sources.

10   9   8   7   6   5   4   3   2   1

To my mother, who raised me in a world of books
as she gave me the gift of being the daughter of a librarian.

To my daughters, who have inspired me to live to heights
I could never have imagined.

And to all those who have so bravely and vulnerably shared
their own stories with me, those who have searched for meaning
within love: nothing has been lost that was meant for you,
and I promise it will all be worth it.

May your heart always remain open to the gift of love,

Kate xx

Contents

Part 3: The Astrology of Twin Flame Relationships

Letter to the Reader

Dear one, the universe has always had your back.

I know that it has not been easy.

That love has only equaled confusion and that amid the strongest storms, you have doubted yourself.

You have doubted your own magnificence, your own divine essence.

You forget that you are a part of this universe as much as the stars are, as much as the sun that beats down hot on your bare skin.

But it is time to come home to yourself.

To return to yourself.

The journey of love is designed to do precisely this.

To help you see that every love, no matter how little time it lasted, no matter how much it broke your heart, was intended to help you become more YOU than you have ever been.

To help you strip away the layers, the masks of all that you never were, so that you could feel your heart beat in sync with the world around you.

Dear one, the universe has always had your back.

Whether you have believed in astrology your whole life — like remnants of a past life clinging onto your soul — or whether you have grown into appreciating the natural rhythms that it carries, astrology has always been there.

The planets and stars are just as undebatable as the fact of you being guided to this moment, to this book, because something deep inside you knows there is more to love.

More to life.

Because even if you have professed otherwise, you have never given up hope. You have never let your internal light become extinguished, no matter how deep the darkness that you walked through.

You have become a warrior in these moments, not just for love, but for the truth.

You know within the fabric of your being that you are meant for more, that love exists. And just because you may not have had love work out in the past, that does not mean it cannot happen in the future.

Still, this knowledge also means you must drop the ways of the world.

Or stop thinking that, because you are restarting your journey at thirty-five, somehow you have done it wrong. Or that, because you are hoping for something you do not see in other relationships, you are crazy.

Crazy for thinking love is real or that, for you, the greatest love will be the one that helps you live out your wild and true nature.

You are not wrong.

Those beliefs are pieces of your soul, wisdom from your ancestors seeped into your bones.

They guide you in this life.

They echo back to a truth that the world has tried to talk you out of.

And no matter how hard you ignore it or try to convince yourself that what you dream of does not exist, you have always returned to your belief in love like a drum beating low and constant in your belly.

Dear one, the universe has always had your back.

The reason that you have been attracted to certain partners, cycles you have had to work through, or relationships that nearly killed your spirit is that they have all been a predetermined part of your path.

The unique astrology you were born with shows you what you are meant to experience and learn in this lifetime.

These experiences have never been random, and nothing has ever been a mistake.

Because there are no failures on this path of love.

There is only you and the lessons you have learned once you reach your forever love.

Astrology is an ancient code, a language handed down through generations of wise ones who studied the stars in hopes of predicting what was to come, in hopes of reaching a destination they did not even know with certainty existed.

And so, this is where you are, dear one.

Relearning your soul's truth and unlearning everything that has stood in the way of you not only becoming the person you are meant to be but also resting in the relationship that you have felt calling to your heart all this time.

The journey of love is really about the self, because until you *truly* know you — until you have accepted your darkness, and have healed those childhood wounds that led to your decisions early on, and have bathed in your own truth while pledging nothing but authenticity — you will keep reencountering the same karmic lessons, since you still need to learn them.

And while you should never stop growing, dear one, you will not be ready to find *the one* until you have mended your broken pieces and faced what you thought was insurmountable pain.

Not because you were ever doing anything wrong, but because you finally got right with yourself.

This rightness opens the divine door of realizing that before anyone can be your one, you must become your own.

Until you have learned not to avoid conversations or intimacy, you will keep pushing away the very thing you want.

Dear one, your forever love does exist.

It has never been based on an illusion or the chasing of something better, but on the internal knowing that love should never make you feel caged. It should never make you feel like you must walk on eggshells or give up the best parts of yourself.

Love will challenge you, make no mistake, but dear one, these challenges are there to slough off parts of you that you no longer need. The bits and pieces of hurt and conditioning have made it impossible to receive what you so deeply desire.

And like a mirror, love will reflect your truth so that finally you can see yourself clearly. Free from the words others spoke of you, free from the burdens of trying to fix everyone else, and free from thinking that there is anything you should be other than your true, authentic self.

Dear one, the universe has always had your back — and it still does.

Even on your darkest days, when you are unsure how to go on, how it will ever feel okay again, the stars are aligned in your favor.

They are conspiring for your greatest good, and all you must do is look up to see that life holds so much more than the fear and doubt that were placed in front of you by those who felt fearful about their own lives.

The cosmos is always waiting for you to read the ancient code of astrology like braille on your heart that's been starved for hope, knowing that once you do, your soul opens to see clearly and choose differently.

Because this is the truth of astrology, of the mystics whose ancient wisdom resides within the deepest part of you. Once you truly see, you can never be blind again.

This book is for you because you are ready and are seeking confirmation for what you already know.

You are ready to open your eyes and see yourself and your relationships clearly.

So you can finally and utterly awaken to see your destiny was always written in the stars.

The First Step to Understanding the Three Loves of Your Life

Regardless of gender, sexual orientation, or even where you call home in this world, a truth exists that unites us: we all fall in love only three times in our lifetime. This is because each love represents a different step of your evolution, a different phase of what it means to use love to understand yourself more deeply.

The first love is the one that looks right.

This is your *soulmate relationship*, although you must still move through personal karma of your own in this union. Often our first comes when we are young, in high school even. It's the idealistic love — the one that seems like something out of the fairy tales we read as children.

This is the love that appeals to what we should be doing for society's — and probably our family's — sake. We enter into it with the belief that this will be our only love, and it doesn't matter if it doesn't feel quite right, or if we find ourselves having to swallow down our personal truths to make it work, because deep down we believe that this is what love is supposed to be.

Because in this type of love, how others view us is more important than how we actually feel.

It's a love that looks right.

The second love is the one that we wished was right.

This is your classic *karmic relationship*, although the karma here is less personal than in the soulmate connection; it is more about your inner child healing from the generational wounds that have been handed down. This is the love that you enter into because your inner child is looking to find validation and worth by being loved by another who has chosen you. While it's common for the soulmate to come first, it's also possible that the karmic will be your first relationship.

The second is supposed to be our hard love — the one that teaches us about who we are and how we want or need to be loved. This is the kind of love that hurts, whether through lies, pain, or manipulation. While you may fall in love only three times, it doesn't mean you will only have one karmic relationship. Many times people will attract multiple karmic partners until the lesson of self-love and healing has finally been learned.

In the karmic relationship, we think we are making choices different from those in our first relationship, but in reality we are still making choices out of the need to learn lessons. Our second love can become a cycle we keep repeating because we think that somehow the ending will be different next time. Yet each time we try, it somehow ends worse than before.

Sometimes the relationship is unhealthy, unbalanced, or narcissistic. There may be emotional, mental, or physical abuse or manipulation; most likely there will be high levels of drama. This is exactly what keeps us addicted to this storyline: it's an emotional roller coaster of extreme highs and lows, and like a junkie trying to get a fix, we stick through the lows with the expectation of the high.

With this kind of love, trying to make it work becomes more important than whether it actually should.

It's simply the love that we wished was right — but was never meant to be.

The third love is the one that lasts.

This is known as your *twin flame*, *divine love*, or even simply a truly healthy relationship.

And this love is the one that we never see coming. The one that usually looks all wrong for us and that destroys any lingering ideals we've been clinging to about what love is supposed to be. This is the love that comes so easily it doesn't seem possible. It's the kind where the connection can't be explained; it knocks us off our feet because we never planned for it. In this connection, you have become aware of what your inner child needs, and while there is never a state of perfection to reach, you are in a process of healing. You understand, more than anything else, that to receive what you've always desired, you must first have given it to yourself.

This is the love where we come together with someone, and it just fits — there aren't any idealized expectations about how each person should be acting, nor is there pressure to become someone else.

We are simply accepted for who we are already — and it shakes us to our core.

It isn't what we envisioned our love would look like, nor does it abide by the rules that we had hoped to play it safe by. It shatters our preconceived notions and shows us that love doesn't have to be how we thought it would be in order to be true.

This is the love that keeps knocking on our door regardless of how long it takes us to answer.

It's the love that just feels right.

To read more about the three loves of your life and their meaning, you can pick up my first book, *You Only Fall in Love Three Times: The Secret Search for Our Twin Flame*, available everywhere.

Preparing for Astrology

Before diving into figuring out what kind of relationship you are in or have been in, you first need to find some necessary astrological information so that you can have it on hand as you move through this book with me. Understanding begins with creating your birth chart, also called your natal chart. This is similar to a life-path map, full of information about all your qualities, desires, and lessons.

When I do astrology readings, I ask for the client's birth time, date, and location, as well as that data for any past, current, or prospective partners they are interested in. In addition, while the karmic relationship is the one that deals with personal and generational karma, it's still always worthwhile to gather your parents' or caregivers' astrology information, as that will help identify patterns that you've been attracting. I've even gone as far back as grandparents, which can be helpful when we get into generational healing.

Many websites offer free birth charts; Café Astrology and Astro-Charts are two that are easy to use. These birth charts represent the zodiac signs the planets were in at the time of your birth and the births of your significant others. All this information becomes the soul map you follow, whether you are consciously aware of it or not.

It is what was written in the stars for you, your life, and all of your relationships.

Part One

THE ASTROLOGY OF
SOULMATE RELATIONSHIPS

When you think of soulmates, do you see them as the highest form of love? A soulmate is part of your soul family, someone you have traveled through lifetimes with and who is an integral part of your journey in this one. The truth is, each of us has multiple soulmates in this life; some are romantic, and others are not.

These are comfortable relationships that often feel like family, even if marriage or children never become part of the equation. That said, a soulmate connection can lead to a feeling that the person you have met is the one, especially because of the similarities between you and them. It will appear you've found the other half of your soul, when in truth, you are simply meeting parts of yourself in another.

This connection serves as a beginning lesson in love and will always be a part of your life. No matter how comfortable it is, though, you eventually realize that you cannot become the person you are meant to be by staying in this relationship. Whether you are lovers, friends, coparents, or even family, a soulmate relationship will need to end so your authentic life can finally begin. Rather than seeing this ending as an ultimate separation, try to embrace it as a chance to grow into the life that is waiting for you.

Your soulmate connection is only the beginning of your love journey, not the final destination. Yet to release this relationship, you must simultaneously be willing to begin the journey of discovering who you truly are.

This is the moment when everything changes — you just don't realize it yet.

Love Isn't Only Logical

Love isn't supposed to make sense — it's supposed to make you feel alive. No matter how well matched two people may look on paper, no matter how logical or commonsensical the pairing may appear, it doesn't determine what the actual relationship will feel like. Choosing a partner purely on the basis of who you always thought you'd marry, who your family approves of, or even who is still single and available isn't the recipe for the love you seek — but it *is* the beginning of discovering what that recipe is.

One of the most interesting aspects of the soulmate relationship is how this partner ends up being so similar to your own self — or at least who you think you are at this point. When you enter your soulmate relationship, you do not truly know who you are or what that even means. Likely, living your truth isn't even on your radar. Many times, it's actually your inner child who is guiding the decisions you're making.

While the soulmate relationship doesn't represent the wounding that the karmic relationship does, it does mirror the conditioning that you experienced as a child; you are merely repeating what you were taught. With the soulmate, you can see how the patterns of your childhood are coming through in your relationships, whether it's through your beliefs of what a relationship is supposed to be or of what a romantic partner represents in your life.

A few years ago, a young woman named Charlotte reached out to me because she'd gone through a horrendous experience of being cheated on and subsequently breaking up with her boyfriend. Charlotte knew that she was being called inward to work on herself in order to attract the type of relationship that she desired. We reflected on the patterns in her relationships and how, ultimately, she felt like she was trying to fit a mold in order to be loved, rather than simply being herself and feeling unconditionally loved for her truth and authenticity. As our work together progressed, she met a new man, Sean, and through our calls and her own willingness and vulnerability, she was able to forge a completely new kind of relationship.

Around the time they were preparing to celebrate their one-year anniversary, Charlotte and I began talking about the astrology of relationships, and she requested that we look at her history. I collected the charts of her parents and her three past exes, going back to her high school sweetheart. The pattern that came through was absolutely incredible and helped give Charlotte much insight into her own journey.

What we discovered was that all three exes had the same South and North Node signs. (I'll get into what the South and North Nodes mean in the chapter "The Lessons of the South Node," but for now just know that they are significant points at the bottom and top of your birth chart.) Moreover, these node signs happened to be the same as those of both her parents, whose charts are shown on the next page. Charlotte realized that in her relationship with her parents, she had become performative to try to earn their love and attention, especially with other siblings in the mix. And, unbeknownst to her, she had been replicating that dynamic as she had continued to attract partners for whom she was performing to earn their love.

While we progress through life, we might think reaching eighteen or graduating from college makes us full-fledged adults. However, in relationships, this time frame is often one where we are still repeating the patterns conditioned into us in our childhood. In the case of Charlotte, she wasn't able to break the pattern until she began to understand what she'd been subconsciously seeking. Once she saw the writing quite clearly in the birth charts, she realized that she was only continuing the same relationship dynamics that she had been exposed to in childhood.

She also found grace for herself and all that she had been through. Instead of adopting the mentality that she was damaged or that "her picker wasn't working properly" — something I frequently hear clients say — she saw how these relationships served an important part of her journey. By realizing that she had to define what love and relationships meant for her, she could start to align herself with what truly would resonate with her. She also realized that she needed to embrace the process of growth that love was meant to bring into her life. In this moment, she began the process of fully stepping into her truth.

CHARLOTTE'S DAD		CHARLOTTE'S MOM	
Sun	Capricorn	Sun	Scorpio
Moon	Aquarius	Moon	Sagittarius
Mercury	Capricorn	Mercury	Sagittarius
Venus	Pisces	Venus	Libra
Mars	Capricorn	Mars	Cancer
Jupiter	Virgo	Jupiter	Libra
Saturn	Cancer	Saturn	Cancer
Uranus	Gemini	Uranus	Gemini
Neptune	Libra	Neptune	Libra
Pluto	Leo	Pluto	Leo
North Node	Capricorn	North Node	Capricorn
South Node	Cancer	South Node	Cancer
Rising	Cancer	Rising	Cancer

The soulmate relationship is built on what appears to be easy to the ego and what will fulfill that inner child desire of pleasing others with your decisions or satisfying what you wished you had experienced. Soulmate relationships are those where you seek to continue what you were conditioned to think love was supposed to be. That means you aren't necessarily making decisions based on your authentic truth; rather, you're trying to make choices that will generate validation similar to what you received or hoped to receive in your childhood. As in Charlotte's story, often in this relationship you're young and have only been exposed to people who live in the same neighborhood or town as you. Your similarities seem enough reason to be together — similar friend groups, similar interests, even birthdays that happen to be close on the calendar. Your soulmate might be the boy next door whom you always had a vision of marrying one day or with whom you even made a pact to do just that if you were both still single in your thirties. But the dynamic goes beyond these superficial similarities; it can manifest as a love in which you both look at the world in a similar way, so it just feels easy. You aren't yet thinking about growth or healing.

The most common element in the astrology charts of soulmates is the lack of complementary energy, which means that these charts contain many similarities. For instance, if you have your sun in Capricorn, your partner may have their moon or Venus in Capricorn.

Complementary energy, which is present in twin flame relationships but typically not in soulmate relationships, speaks to a balance. For example, if you are introverted, your partner's extroversion encourages you to step outside your comfort zone; or if your partner is constantly active, your more relaxed presence guides them to be more in the moment. With complementary energy, you are seeking someone who can benefit and bring balance to your life rather than being simply just like yourself.

In a soulmate relationship, it can feel like you're with your best friend because there are little to no challenges, but that also is why there is rarely any growth. Instead of the dynamic evolution that occurs within the twin-flame healthy love relationship (which we'll cover in detail in part 3), in the soulmate relationship you end up being forced to choose between staying in it or leaving in order to grow, even if that means growing apart from someone you thought you would always be with and perhaps still love.

To make the choice to part ways from your soulmate is the beginning of the journey to learn who you genuinely are and how to fall in love with all your pieces.

You Don't Really Want to Date Yourself

In astrology, your sun, moon, and rising signs are commonly considered the "big three." But when it comes to the astrology of soulmate relationships, your sun, moon, Saturn, and Mercury are the most impactful. What you end up doing in a soulmate relationship is attracting someone who is like you, not necessarily someone who complements or even challenges you. The sun and moon represent core parts of who you are, not just your personality but also what you need. Mercury governs how you communicate with others and how you need to be spoken to, significantly impacting a romantic relationship. Saturn, though, is the key here, as it represents the type of karma that every soulmate relationship possesses. This relationship is where you try to recreate what you are told love *should* be instead of listening to your authentic self, because you do not even know that is an option yet. In the soulmate relationship, you're following the blueprint that family or society has given you, instead of stopping to ask yourself, "What do I need from love and a relationship?"

The soulmate relationship is categorized by attracting a partner who is similar to yourself, because only in this connection are you both given the opportunity to grow beyond what is expected and into your authentic self — and the love that is meant for you. The soulmate relationship can show up in a couple of different ways in the astrology charts. The first is that you will both share the same Saturn sign; for instance, Saturn may be in Libra in both your and your partner's astrology charts. The soulmate relationship can also be marked by similarities in your sun, moon, and Mercury signs.

While having the same Saturn sign is a classic example of the soulmate relationship, this relationship can show up differently for some depending on what they are meant to learn. The reason that Saturn becomes so significant is that this planet represents your personal karma and lessons in this lifetime. So in the soulmate union, you attract someone with the same Saturn sign so that you can recognize who you are apart from what you have been taught to be.

This idea of eventually transitioning out of your soulmate relationship is a relatively new phenomenon in human evolution. You can see this in reviewing the charts of your parents and grandparents: the majority stayed within their soulmate or Saturn relationships. Yet it has become more acceptable to grow and evolve personally, and so a similar evolution now takes place in romantic relationships, which is why soulmate relationships serve as just the beginning point. Every relationship has its own karma to work through, simply because there is always more to learn. Although the soulmate union represents the karma of authenticity and truth, the karmic relationship helps you to heal your childhood wounds so that you can learn to finally receive your healthy love in the twin flame or divine love connection.

This is where the belief that love should be logical can be felt the most strongly, because you are choosing how your partner can fit into your story instead of who they or, more importantly, who you authentically are. But it is also the first step onto the path of realizing that what seems like the perfect relationship is only an illusion. Your soulmate might be someone who your family and friends all approve of, someone who even looks great with you — but that doesn't mean they're someone you can have a lasting, conscious, growth-oriented relationship with.

Once, when I was barely twenty and involved in one of my lesson relationships, I walked out of a restaurant with my boyfriend. I think we even did that very nineties thing of putting our hands in the back pockets of each other's jeans as we crossed through the shadows of the streetlights. As we were walking, a stranger stopped us and told us that aesthetically we made such a great couple.

Now, as I write this, I laugh because we could have looked like brother and sister — something that's also common in soulmate relationships. But I also shake my head because I remember how amazing that comment felt at the time. As if being physically compatible with someone was the highest compliment.

When you are enmeshed within your soulmate relationship, in many ways you're hoping to blend in. You're hoping to just do what everyone else is doing without creating too many ripples in the status quo; you don't want to risk being tossed off anyone's island. When you are just beginning your journey of the soul, your sense of self relies upon the social acceptance of others. The last thing you want to do is make a romantic decision that could put that in jeopardy.

Yet love isn't about following the rules or making the logical choice others are encouraging you to make. And so eventually you realize that looking good doesn't mean much at all if it doesn't actually feel good. Being with someone who is so similar to you loses its appeal as you realize it's like dating yourself. You might have that indescribable feeling of something not being right, yet you're not able to describe what is wrong because you're just starting out on the journey to discover who you are.

This is precisely what makes the soulmate relationship so challenging to move on from. Many times clients say, "I think that I can stay, I think it is good enough." But love isn't supposed to be "good enough." It's supposed to continually inspire you to become better, to love better, and to embrace all that life is meant to be.

To live small is to think that "good enough" will ever satisfy you without taking the leap of faith to see how big, how amazing, how refreshing life can be — even if you choose to have a small cabin in the forest surrounded by the silence of the trees. Living small doesn't necessarily mean that you live in a modest home, just as living big doesn't necessarily mean you have millions or mansions. Rather, the size of how you're living comes from how expansive you allow your soul to be. And that is based on what you believe to be true about life.

When we're in the soulmate relationship, we all are living small, simply because we haven't yet opened that elusive door to our soul to discover who we truly are. Yet when you make that choice, when you answer the knock from the universe, everything changes, because no longer are you moving through life asleep. You are wide awake and committed to never missing a single moment again.

A few years ago, I received a call from a gentleman named Kenneth, who was feeling confused and conflicted about his relationship with his longtime girlfriend, Leora. Kenneth and Leora met when they were young. They were from the same town, and their families knew of each other. It was their sameness that had drawn them together, and that was echoed in their birthdays: despite being a few years apart, one was born on January 10, and the other on January 11.

KENNETH	
Sun	Capricorn
Moon	Gemini
Mercury	Capricorn
Venus	Sagittarius
Mars	Aries
Jupiter	Pisces
Saturn	Sagittarius
Uranus	Sagittarius
Neptune	Capricorn
Pluto	Scorpio
North Node	Aries
South Node	Libra
Rising	Aries

LEORA	
Sun	Capricorn
Moon	Sagittarius
Mercury	Capricorn
Venus	Aquarius
Mars	Aries
Jupiter	Sagittarius
Saturn	Sagittarius
Uranus	Sagittarius
Neptune	Capricorn
Pluto	Scorpio
North Node	Cancer
South Node	Capricorn
Rising	Aries

Kenneth and Leora began their relationship, as many soulmates do, with the intention of marrying, creating a home, and having children together. Yet something kept calling Kenneth away from the relationship. He proposed twice but also broke the engagement twice, as he couldn't quite commit to Leora in the ways she desired. To make matters more complicated, they had a child together and even lived together for more than a decade. But in true soulmate relationship fashion, Kenneth never felt satisfied; he always felt himself drifting away.

As we began talking, he expressed that the relationship was good enough, and while he tried his best to show up and be consistent, because the partnership didn't offer him healing or growth, he never felt really connected to Leora or the life that he had promised her. He felt a great deal of guilt identifying his truth, but he also had the desire to experience life, to grow. He struggled with facing the reality that he wouldn't be able to evolve within this connection.

The story of Leora and Kenneth is that of picture-perfect soulmates: shared familial conditioning, a level of sameness, and even almost-shared birthdays. But while the similarities were what initially attracted Kenneth, they ultimately became what caused him to pull away. The relationship with Leora offered no complementary energy, no balance. Instead, as he came to realize, he was dating himself all of those years.

In looking at the astrology charts of Kenneth, Leora, and their parents, it became clear to me that, unknowingly, Kenneth and Leora were also repeating what they were taught to believe love was in childhood. They were attracted to each other not only because they were incredibly similar but also because Kenneth had similarities to the charts of Leora's parents, just as she had similarities to his. Still, as in other soulmate relationships, the question was whether the relationship would ever get bad enough to motivate them to end it or instead would always remain just good enough that neither would want to venture out of the comfort zone of their childhood conditioning.

Eventually it was Kenneth who came to see that the reason he was sabotaging the connection was that ultimately good enough wasn't actually good enough anymore. He made the choice to separate, not necessarily to jump into a new love, but to find out who he authentically was without the influence of any romantic partner in his life. This is a common theme when soulmates end their relationship: a new love isn't necessarily something they're looking for, but instead, the connection with their own divine self is.

Saturn Is Your Soulmate

Saturn, known as the Lord of Time and Karma, is a planet that helps you to set boundaries and also to understand that in order to progress to that next chapter of your life, you must finally comprehend the lessons that are a part of your growth. In this, the soulmate relationship mirrors back to you what you need to learn to be able to authentically be yourself and create the life that resonates with your soul. This is perfectly illustrated in the charts of Kenneth and Leora, with them sharing a Saturn placement in Sagittarius.

Saturn is also called the father of the zodiac, and so I look to it as offering the master lesson that we all need to move through to be able to change our behavior and become the person we are meant to be, just like in childhood, when we learn the most important lessons at the hands of our parents or caregivers. There is a big difference between being in your Saturn lesson, refusing to learn it, and at last clearly seeing what has been the truth all along. Saturn isn't only your karmic lesson but is also involved in beginning to heal the conditioning or even wounds that you experienced early in life so that you can step into your truth more fully.

Relationships that have Saturn in the same sign are very challenging to get out of, because they tempt you with everything you thought you wanted, though they are not consistently healthy, or they bring up the deep desire to continually fix the relationship or even the partner. This is why your own perception of what love should be becomes the karma within the soulmate relationship. The setup appears to offer the so-called perfect relationship, but in actuality this relationship is only reflecting a singular step in your own growth.

That said, when you are comparing your chart to your past, current, or prospective partner's and you notice that you have the same Saturn placement, it isn't an invitation to run the other way, but rather to be aware that this may be more of a lesson relationship than one meant to last forever. While some have called this aspect of astrology a cheat sheet for relationships, you can't bypass the lesson and expect to receive the blessing.

Your Saturn sign points the way to the major lesson you will learn in your lifetime. This is one that shows up primarily in romantic relationships, though it may also be connected to your childhood wounds. What zodiac sign your Saturn is in will signify how that specific lesson looks for you.

Saturn is not a one-size-fits-all planet. While its lessons all incorporate healing and the embodiment of a greater truth, each lesson is determined by its zodiac sign placement and how it will require you to grow to reach the best version of yourself.

To understand your Saturn sign is to also accept what will be most challenging in this life and what will keep presenting itself until you finally learn it. For example, if your Saturn is in Libra, you will continue to sacrifice internal peace for the external illusion of it until you learn the lesson that you must prioritize your peace within.

Saturn is considered by many astrologers a difficult planet, one that can invoke fear or anxiety, but that's not its true nature. Saturn is a compassionate guide for your personal lessons, and it also offers the reassurance of divine timing, which is always at play in your life. Saturn becomes challenging only when the lessons are not yet visible or are continually ignored. As with anything in life, when you understand the process that's at work, it becomes easier and actually brings a peace that can help you find acceptance and hope for all that is to come.

Fire Saturn Signs (Aries, Leo, and Sagittarius)

Affirmation of Authenticity: *I fully accept myself.*

Saturn in any of the fire signs carries the lesson of learning to fully accept yourself as you are so that you may begin to lessen your need to receive validation from others in your life. Often in your soulmate or Saturn relationship, you will try to change yourself in an effort to gain the love and external validation that you were deprived of early in life.

While healing will inevitably bring a balance into your life, you must also learn the difference between doing what society believes is right versus following your own internal barometer for what feels right to you. You have an enormous ability to create and to practice boldness when it matters most, but to fully step into that power you must learn that you already have everything you need within yourself to attract and create the life that resonates with your deepest truth. Once you realize this, you will no longer continue relationships for the sake of the status quo or for appearances, and instead you'll be let loose to discover what truly sets your heart on fire.

Earth Saturn Signs (Taurus, Virgo, and Capricorn)

Affirmation of Authenticity: *I am able to keep myself safe.*

As a Saturn earth sign, you hold the ability to create a sense of safety and stability within any area of your life — but this is something that you will first be challenged to learn. Initially, you connect your sense of personal stability to upholding your comfort zone. In essence, you are relying on external factors to feel safe instead of seeing that safety is a feeling you can nurture within yourself.

Once you realize that trying to keep an unsatisfying relationship together or make decisions on the basis of your family's approval doesn't produce that sense of safety you desire, you then begin the journey of operating from more faith and self-trust. By cultivating a feeling of safety within yourself, you not only continue to evolve but also never have to fear change ever again.

Air Saturn Signs (Gemini, Libra, and Aquarius)

Affirmation of Authenticity: *I am confident in my independence.*

If your Saturn is in an air sign, it means you will be learning your independence, and with that also comes the understanding of how to remain your individual self even in relationship with another. Many times, Saturn air signs rely on their partner to feel free, financially abundant, or confident enough to pursue their dreams, because they are outsourcing how they see themselves onto their romantic partner. Through the journey of the soulmate relationship, a dramatic shift often occurs as Saturn air signs become able to recognize their talents and ability to live the life they have always wanted.

Once a Saturn air sign can feel confident in their independence, they are also ready to practice the art of interdependence, where they can merge their life with another's without fear of losing themself once again. Instead of bending to the will or ideas of your partner, you will be able to remain strong, to advocate for your needs, and to recognize that you don't have to appear weak or needy in order to receive the love that you desire. Being confident in your independence allows you to attract a partner who will support you in accomplishing all you've ever dreamed of.

Water Saturn Signs (Cancer, Scorpio, and Pisces)

Affirmation of Authenticity: *I practice healthy boundaries by honoring my emotional needs.*

Individuals with Saturn in one of the water signs often need to learn that emotionality doesn't equate to weakness but instead can represent the most powerful force there is. Having Saturn in a water sign brings about the realization that setting emotional boundaries is the only way to have your needs met, a lesson that often takes the shape of feeling like you're being taken advantage of or continuously landing in unreciprocal relationships. To learn your Saturn lesson, you need to go through the process of realizing that until you prioritize your emotions, no one else will either.

Once you begin to emerge from this place of feeling like everything you've been through is unfair, you will start to take back power over how you allow others to treat you. This epitomizes the idea that what you will allow is what will continue. As you begin to practice healthy boundaries, you also start to feel more autonomous in your life. Instead of needing others to create boundaries for you or feeling less than because a partner didn't honor what you deserve, you will realize that the love you have to share is a gift you will give only to those who have shown themselves worthy.

The Attraction of Your Sun and Moon

There is a significant difference between a relationship based on who you are projecting to the world and who you are when the rest of the world falls silent. The sun is the center of our solar system, and in its bright boldness, it reflects your external qualities. Your sun sign represents how you are seen by others, but this only means it is how you are perceived and not who you are when you don't have to be anything other than yourself. While important, especially in soulmate relationships, it is just one element of many in your birth chart.

Oftentimes, I will see a client with an Aquarius sun, for example, yet they don't necessarily fall within the stereotype of this sign because their moon sign, their Venus, or their Mercury is giving them other characteristics. To take another example, I am a Pisces sun, yet while I am romantic to a fault (a trait Pisces is known for), I don't come across as a typical emotional water sign because I am also a leading air element. That means that I have the majority of my planet placements in air signs, so the qualities of air, such as being very communicative and open-minded, override my water qualities. Your leading element actually has the same significance in your chart that your rising sign has.

If I were to fully embrace only my Pisces sun, it would define certain types of partners that I would work best with. However, recognizing that I am a leading air element, I actually live my life more from the energy of air, so I need to choose my relationships accordingly. Each of us has great depth. To choose a relationship that is in alignment with who we are, we need to fully understand our own soul first. Otherwise what we choose won't be a reflection of what we need or even what will complement our lives.

The sun is only one part of a complex map of your soul; it does not dictate true compatibility or growth potential. Think of it like a magnet: two north poles will only repel, while a north and a south pole will create such a strong pull that it can be difficult to separate them — and isn't that what you desire? A connection so strong that nothing can break it; a connection that time will lie down and be still for?

Often what you truly need is someone who balances your weaknesses with their strengths, not someone who brings the very same qualities to the table that you already have. Just imagine if everyone attending a dinner party brought the same dish. There would be no variety, no tantalizing combination of flavors — just like in a soulmate relationship, which is why, after a period of time, you begin to crave more.

In soulmate relationships, you will often see similar sun and moon signs. Even if they aren't exactly the same, there will be a crossover or commonality with other placements in the charts. Again, it's a case of like attracting like, being drawn to the perceived ease of moving through life with someone who appears to be the same. You don't yet know that you will never be able to evolve into any other version of yourself while remaining in that relationship. The story of Kenneth and Leora that I shared is a perfect case in point. Essentially, they were too similar to ever be each other's catalyst of growth.

Attracting someone who is the same as you not only is repeating the patterns or conditioning of childhood, but is also a message that you are attracting a mirror for the sole purpose of being able to see yourself more deeply. Each relationship will ultimately mirror a different part of yourself back to you. The soulmate relationship is meant to show you your beliefs, conditioning, and needs more clearly. The karmic relationship (which we'll get into in part 2) points toward the wounds you need to heal. As you journey through each relationship, you are moving ever closer to embracing your authentic truth, which is what paves the way for drawing the third type of love, the twin flame relationship, into your life.

While your sun rules how others perceive you, your moon governs your authentic nature. Your moon sign reigns over your emotional self; because of this, it is also often where your truth blossoms from. It's the part of you that isn't apparent from your appearance or how you live your life, the part of you that is always working behind the scenes to make choices for your highest self.

One of the purposes of your soulmate journey is to learn that and then recognize how to embrace this quiet part of you instead of indulging in maintaining appearances. This is the journey of going deeper, not just in love but, more importantly, within yourself. While the attraction between the sun and moon is one that bonds the connection in familiarity, as I've said, it's not one that offers the possibility for growth. Whether you intend it or not, ultimately this union will feel limiting to you.

When you reflect on your life, you will realize you have outgrown countless aspects of it, from the fashions of your teenage years to how you liked to spend your time or what you thought you would be when you grew up. So it's no surprise that eventually you have to outgrow your soulmate connection in order to fully embrace the bigger journey into your truth and the fate that was written in the stars for you.

Alignment

Even if it seems you and your partner are on the same page about your union's purpose, the reality is that you may each be experiencing a totally different type of connection at any one time. A feeling of connectedness comes through in many conversations I have when clients say they are beginning to think their relationship is a soulmate relationship. Meanwhile, their partner is convinced they are twin flames.

While any disagreement can be challenging, this one, especially for soulmates, can be incredibly difficult because it brings guilt and triggers into the relationship. But these also serve a purpose.

Cassidy reached out to me because she thought her partner, Jackie, was a soulmate connection and not her forever relationship. They had been together for years and had children together. Still, something kept nagging at Cassidy that this was not the relationship she was supposed to be in for the rest of her life. She could not find anything specifically wrong, but something did not feel right.

Making matters worse was that Jackie was confident they were twin flames. This confidence made Cassidy question herself. She felt guilty for not feeling as committed to Jackie as Jackie had hoped she would be. Of course, these issues became part of their relationship's purpose: Cassidy needed to learn to listen to herself above all others. Even if challenging or difficult, she needed to follow her true path; this soulmate relationship was where she could learn how to do that.

Balance Is Everything

An important lesson you learn in the soulmate relationship is that what is best for you is not what is most *like* you but, rather, what *complements* you. Because, as I say to clients and as we've already discussed, no one wants to date themselves.

In Cassidy and Jackie's case, they were remarkably similar. Their sun signs — which represent how they are seen by others and the choices they make externally in their lives — were the same. Their sun signs show how they move within the world, but they do not accurately reflect who they are internally.

We all have an external self that others believe us to be and an internal one that is our true self. Soulmate relationships appeal to that external self because we have not yet figured out that who we appear to be to others may not actually be who we are on an authentic level.

As an example, below are the charts for Cassidy and Jackie.

CASSIDY	
Sun	Sagittarius
Moon	Virgo
Mercury	Sagittarius
Venus	Capricorn
Mars	Scorpio
Jupiter	Aries
Saturn	Sagittarius
Uranus	Sagittarius
Neptune	Capricorn
Pluto	Scorpio
North Node	Pisces
South Node	Virgo
Rising	Pisces

JACKIE	
Sun	Sagittarius
Moon	Gemini
Mercury	Scorpio
Venus	Sagittarius
Mars	Scorpio
Jupiter	Aries
Saturn	Sagittarius
Uranus	Sagittarius
Neptune	Capricorn
Pluto	Scorpio
North Node	Cancer
South Node	Capricorn
Rising	Sagittarius

You can see a lot of Sagittarius, fire energy, present in both charts. The same dominant energy — whether fire, water, earth, or air — is commonly found in the charts of soulmate relationships. So there are many similarities between the two individuals, but not necessarily the balance of energy that is present in our twin flame relationship.

If you compare the two charts, you can see, as I mentioned earlier, that the sun sign is the same. When two people share the same sun sign, they are attracted to what they perceive they need to get or be within a relationship. However, they may not know what they need until the relationship develops over time, which of course is when one or both people start to think of ending the connection. This is an attraction based on their own lack of truth and the conditioning from others, instead of being the place to attract someone who will continue to challenge them in the best ways possible over the course of their lifetime.

Try comparing your birth chart to those of the people who have entered your life, especially romantic partners, and see how their sun sign appeals to the various parts of you. This is the journey of being the person you were told or expected to be versus being the soul that you truly are.

In the case of Cassidy and Jackie, with both charts having such a great deal of Sagittarius energy, you can see that instead of Cassidy being attracted to a complementary partner based on her own sun, and Mercury placements, she fell for the external qualities that Jackie's sun and Venus represented.

Her external self, Sagittarius, was attracted to Jackie's sun, and Venus in Sagittarius because that's how she thought she should be loved — instead of how she needs to *be*. These charts represent a relationship that looks like it would be a good fit because they contain so many similar aspects, but the partnership lacks what each truly needs from love, which the Venus and North Node placements represent.

This is also where my reading differs from much of what you will read about compatibility. Many standard astrology readings on relationships are looking only at soulmate relationships, neglecting to see the larger picture and healing purpose in the relationships you choose. In astrology, the North Node represents the fate you are moving toward once you learn the karmic lessons from your South Node and Saturn placements.

In the case of Cassidy and Jackie, while there are astrological markers that make this an important learning relationship, what is most crucial to look at is how Cassidy's sun sign is mirrored in multiple placements within Jackie's chart. Your soulmate Venus sign is where you can see if you are leaning into what is authentic for you or if you are just being attracted to what feels familiar. The latter is exactly what Cassidy's chart reveals. It also shows that even though they are together in a relationship, their lessons differ. Cassidy, like so many going through life, learned to identify with whatever obvious traits she was aware of or others pointed out to her (again, represented by her sun sign).

To be able to recognize that the soulmate relationship limits you, you first must see where you are limiting your own self, and you cannot do that without seeing it reflected back to you. Each relationship is challenging to move beyond, but the soulmate relationship often carries the additional weight of causing you to feel that you are disappointing family or friends if you do decide to end it.

The soulmate relationship presents the opportunity for you to remove the veil of who you have been conditioned to be and instead allow the layers of your true self to be revealed to you. It's the relationship where for the first time in your life you stake a claim in your own truth, you begin to trust yourself, and you realize that there is no point in making decisions based on worrying about being kicked off an island you now know you're not meant to remain on.

Every relationship that we choose is for a purpose, but, as I've said, that does not mean it is necessarily meant to last forever. In the case of soulmates, it is not the differences that become the challenge but the sameness, because within that space you become boxed into a particular version of yourself.

Your soulmate relationship is not yet reflective of your diverse, wild, authentic self because you are still learning to put those pieces together. While there are obviously many distinct aspects to the astrology chart, when you are in your soulmate relationship, looking at the sun, moon, and Mercury signs is essential to learning what you were unconsciously attracted to in your partner.

Cassidy was attracted to Jackie's Sagittarian sun, and Venus, even though this attraction spoke only to one part of her and did not account for her own unique needs, which are represented by Cassidy's Venus and moon placements.

As in Cassidy's example, your sun sign will become unconsciously attracted to another's sun, moon, Mercury, or Venus placement because something about them will register as familiar to you. Yet you will learn, in the course of the relationship, that your attraction does not mean this partner is able to love you in the ways that you need. People often think karmic relationships are the only type of soul connection that teaches a lesson, but every relationship teaches us something we need to learn about ourselves — even if the lesson is to start the process of asking yourself what love means to you, apart from all you have been told it is supposed to be.

Which is exactly the purpose of this connection. You need your soulmate relationship; you need to see how your sun sign is attracted to the sameness of another person to start realizing that you need more, simply because you are far more than your sun sign. You are vast and creative and have a multitude of dimensions that make up your beautiful, authentic self.

When you come to understand the lesson, you understand the purpose of this relationship in your life, and then you become ready for the next chapter in your own love story.

Mercury and Speaking Your Truth

Truth is love.

Speaking your authentic truth is essential in any relationship you have. In soulmate chart comparisons, the placement of Mercury, the planet of communication, is one of the most important aspects to consider, because no matter how hard you might wish this person to be your forever love, your ability to discover and articulate your truth will create separation.

Mercury is the planet that rules your thoughts and how you communicate them. It is known as the master of the mind, and it dictates everything from your own self-talk to how you communicate with the world. In relationships, communication is a hugely important piece — not just communication about the essential things, like what direction the relationship is going, but also the energy with which you are conveying your thoughts and needs to your partner.

Mercury placements that work cohesively with your partner change the entire connection, just as Mercury placements that fuel arguments or unmet needs do. When it comes to soulmate relationships, even if other placements are the same, it's common for your Mercury placement to be different from your soulmate's. This actually aids the ultimate purpose of the soulmate relationship, which is to find and express your truth.

We are taught to mourn relationships when they end, to see it all as heartbreak and sadness, but in the case of soulmate endings, it is always more of a transition, and the ending also marks a new beginning. It may not always be easy to focus on the positives of an ending, but when it comes to Mercury and your soulmate connection, it is important to consider the benefits the separation may bring.

Mercury is the planet that is retrograde most frequently in astrology, meaning it appears to be moving backward in the sky as it begins a new cycle. This retrograde cycle occurs anywhere from three to five times a year. Rather than seeing Mercury retrograde as a time when everything will go wrong, as popular culture incorrectly has you believe, it is a chance to make things right — to tap into the ability to reflect on your truth and the words that you are speaking, which will go into the creation of the life that you dream of.

When soulmates have contrasting Mercury placements — for instance, Mercury in Scorpio and Mercury in Sagittarius, in the case of Jackie and Cassidy — it means that there will not be a meeting of the minds. And as much as it will feel like a soulmate connection, the union is not truly between the souls.

Mercury helps you to understand the difference between a partner who complements you and one who seems destined to never understand you.

You Cannot Fix What Is Not Meant to Work

Going back to Cassidy and Jackie's charts, we see that each has their Mercury in vastly different zodiac signs. Mercury is in far-reaching Sagittarius for Cassidy, and for Jackie, it is in intense Scorpio. The fact that they are in a fire and water sign, respectively, does not matter as much, because different elements can bring balance to each other.

For example, Sagittarius is one of the zodiac's most philosophical signs. Sagittarius prioritizes truth, knowledge, learning, and the freedom to explore life. Scorpio is an intense water sign known for being passionate and obsessive at times, hiding their true feelings deep beneath the surface, and needing such a profound level of commitment that it can sometimes create the feeling of suffocation for their partner.

Mercury in these two placements results in two vastly different communication styles. The Sagittarius partner would be open to innovative ideas and seeing things from various perspectives to learn more about life, whereas the Scorpio individual would tend to believe they were always right and would be reluctant to entertain new or untraditional ideas. This is how two people's Mercury placements can make all the difference in a relationship: no one wants to spend their whole life feeling like they are constantly trying to explain themselves.

When conversations about growth and life come up, each person dreams about their future differently.

Let us take Cassidy's chart and compare it now to that of her prospective new partner, Marina.

These two charts (shown on the next page) look less similar than the previous two, especially in their Mercury placements. The real difference is in how they work together.

Marina has her Mercury in Aquarius, a zodiac sign that expresses itself through freedom and learning. The rebel with a cause, Aquarius would appeal to Sagittarius's desire to explore life and learn freely. In this case, the air element of Aquarius for Marina's Mercury placement would fuel the flames of Cassidy's Mercury in fiery Sagittarius, encouraging both of them to communicate openly and transparently, without judgment or pressure.

Both of these placements of Mercury represent a greater desire for freedom, autonomy, and breaking the status quo than Marina and Cassidy possessed. In astrology, partnership is never about having to be the same; instead, we are looking for how to complement or reach greater heights within the relationship than what we can accomplish alone or with someone who is committed to misunderstanding us.

CASSIDY	
Sun	Sagittarius
Moon	Virgo
Mercury	Sagittarius
Venus	Capricorn
Mars	Scorpio
Jupiter	Aries
Saturn	Sagittarius
Uranus	Sagittarius
Neptune	Capricorn
Pluto	Scorpio
North Node	Pisces
South Node	Virgo
Rising	Pisces

MARINA	
Sun	Pisces
Moon	Aquarius
Mercury	Aquarius
Venus	Capricorn
Mars	Libra
Jupiter	Scorpio
Saturn	Libra
Uranus	Sagittarius
Neptune	Sagittarius
Pluto	Scorpio
North Node	Sagittarius
South Node	Gemini
Rising	Virgo

Similar Venus placements can be helpful, because Venus rules how you love and need to be loved. Similar Mercury signs, on the other hand, can offer little to no balance in the relationship, resulting in partners staying within their comfort zones or conditioned belief systems. Between being too similar and too opposite, your own pendulum must find balance. That balance looks like speaking your feelings effortlessly yet still being challenged to reflect on your own process.

Many times in my work with couples, I see people who are trying to repair a connection or marriage. While you can work on communication, quality time, or intimacy, often what people seek when they approach a counselor is to make the relationship into something it never was.

They are trying to get back to the space before each person grew and changed, to somehow feel like they are once again aligned or have that mysterious element of chemistry and attraction. But in love, when you have simply outgrown a connection, it's not a matter of trying to get back what you imagine you once had. Your task is to accept where you are in this moment, so that you can begin to make decisions your future self will thank you for. Because once you've outgrown a connection, there is no amount of romantic dates, flowers, or even sex that will make you feel aligned once again.

The soulmate relationship lasts only if you both stay the same. Realistically, this is an impossible concept, as change is the only given in life. But it is scary to speak the truth, and it can be terrifying to think that you are going to make choices your family may not agree with. Yet to speak your truth, even as you may struggle to trust within it, is the only path forward, because while you can't fix what isn't meant to work, you can grow into what will.

What Cassidy struggled with most was that she still loved Jackie. She didn't understand how she could love her, take on the weight of potentially breaking her heart, and still feel this desire to move in a new direction with her life. But I told her that the truth was, seldom do relationships end because love is no longer there. While love is important, it is not everything.

We can love someone for who they've become in our lives. We can love them because they've helped us grow, because they've always been there for us, or because they were our safe space when we didn't feel safe with ourselves. We can love them as parents and as friends. There are a million ways to love someone — and still it doesn't necessarily mean that a romantic relationship is possible or wise.

If you are struggling with the very same thing, the best thing to do is embrace it. Send them love. Wish them well. Be amazing coparents, friends, or family members. Embrace the fact that rarely do two people in a relationship mutually want to end it at the same time. Because in this case you are the one who has that knowledge, now love them enough to set them free.

Do so without procrastinating. (It only gets harder.) Do so without unconsciously acting out in hopes they'll end it. Do it in the moment you know your truth, and do it with love. Love doesn't mean hanging on; it's realizing that it can exist even in the space of growing apart.

Here's the thing. As much as you feel called to take this new turn in your soul's path, your soulmate is being led to do so as well, so that they can become the person they are meant to be and attract a love that is in alignment with who they are. To do something new, something scary, is the risk your soul will always ask you to take.

It is the journey of the warrior.

In Paulo Coelho's novel *The Alchemist*, an Andalusian shepherd goes off on a journey by himself to discover his greatest treasure. So too will you have to venture away from what is known to learn that the treasure you seek outside of yourself is in fact the one found within. In love and especially in soulmate relationships, where it is all about reaching the milestones that love is supposed to represent, such as marriage and children, this idea that what you seek outside of yourself is what you must wake up to within yourself is foreign.

Mercury not only governs your thoughts — it also governs your awareness. You cannot have a moment of great awakening without this planet. Mercury represents the ultimate choice in your soulmate connection to either express your truth and leave this relationship or spend a lifetime trying to translate your soul to someone who does not speak the same language.

The bittersweet beauty of the soulmate relationship is that you finally learn you do have a choice. And with it comes a learned responsibility to yourself: to honor your own truth above all else.

Mercury in the Zodiac Signs

Mercury in Aries

Your Truth Lesson Affirmation: *I trust in my instincts and truth yet am open to seeing things differently.*

In Aries, Mercury works rapidly and passionately. Because of your determination, you feel confident about your words; however, you can also be prone to regret. This occurs because you rush to express something, then are disappointed with the results. You are only responsible for expressing your truth — what comes of it is out of your control — but you might need to strategize before trying again. You may be more argumentative than most, but your words can also be productive banter, which helps you develop exciting ideas and ways of relating within a connection. In relationships, monitor how much your need to be right fuels your words or actions, as self-sabotage can be a real thing. Even though you forgive and move on easily, your partner may not.

The deciding factors in staying together (or not) may be found in how well you exercise caution before speaking and how well your partner can hold space for all you move through without taking your sometimes brash words personally. Let your relationship be a space where your truth is honored, yet you also feel challenged to see things from a different perspective. Embrace your ability to be direct and trust that this is one of your greatest strengths, even if others try to convince you it's not.

Most Complementary Mercury Placements: Gemini, Leo, and Scorpio

Mercury in Taurus

Your Truth Lesson Affirmation: *I will continually advocate for myself to create a life of security and abundance.*

With your Mercury in Taurus, you are slow to argue and often need extended time to process conversations or feelings before you feel ready to speak about them. This is part of your lesson of advocating for yourself without fearing that you will be punished. As much as you crave peace, learning that your sense of security is to be found within yourself lets you step into a space of greater authenticity in your relationship. While a relationship should feel stable, you also need to learn that no matter what happens in love, stability is something that you create for yourself. Getting to the root of an issue is crucial so you can communicate what will help create a solid foundation for you in the relationship.

That said, while processing is a good thing, it is essential not to wait too long; otherwise, you tend to become resentful of your partner and even of yourself at times. Stubbornness is also a factor: it might show up as you not wanting to speak about something you think your lover should already know or as you simply being afraid to share. Knowing when to speak up and what to compromise on will be key to creating a long-lasting, healthy relationship.

Most Complementary Mercury Placements: Cancer, Virgo, and Capricorn

Mercury in Gemini

Your Truth Lesson Affirmation: *I trust myself to know my truth and will communicate it clearly and authentically with those in my life.*

One of the most significant issues Mercury in Gemini faces is that with so many ideas popping in your head at once, it can be hard to know which you should run with or even speak up about. Your task is to identify your own truth versus others' feelings or desires. You can debate every side of a topic, but that doesn't mean all those arguments are really your truth. When it comes to emotions, you must make sure they are not fleeting before you blurt them out. Ask yourself if something that is arising is permanent or only temporary; avoid acting on something that is simply a phase you, or you and your lover, are moving through. When you become more solid in your own truth, not only will you feel more grounded, but you'll also be in the position to create a more stable relationship.

You tend to change your mind more than most because of your sense of duality, embodied in Gemini, the sign of the twins. Having a partner who is flexible and does not take things personally is crucial for you to be able to grow together. You tend to want to talk things out a great deal with friends or family, but talking about every aspect of your relationship with people outside of it can harm the connection, especially if you want to stay together. Being mindful of what you share with others can strengthen your relationship.

Most Complementary Mercury Placements: Capricorn, Aquarius, and Aries

Mercury in Cancer

Your Truth Lesson Affirmation: *I am committed to a truth of deep emotional honesty, and I trust that I am safe to share it with those in my inner circle.*

Feelings are your top priority if you have Mercury in nurturing Cancer, as is the well-being of everyone close to you. Separating your feelings from those of people around you will ensure that what you choose to communicate will be yours and not theirs. When talking issues through with a partner, make sure you take accountability for your own feelings instead of placing blame or responsibility on them to make you feel a certain way. While a healthy relationship should add to your happiness and even your stability, it shouldn't be the sole source of these things. Get to know who you are apart from your relationship so that you feel more secure in sharing your truth. Hiding out is a normal response when you feel overwhelmed; it can give you time to process whether you are reacting to the truth or to a projection.

If you do feel challenged and need space, letting your partner know this instead of simply going silent can go a long way toward nurturing a healthy connection. There is a great depth of emotions with this sign, so you may find yourself expressing love through acts of service; having a partner who values that is important. You need a partner to hold a great deal of emotional space for you and to validate your feelings, even if they disagree. Equally, they need for you to give them the same consideration without interpreting what they share as a threat to the relationship.

Most Complementary Mercury Placements: Taurus, Virgo, and Scorpio

Mercury in Leo

Your Truth Lesson Affirmation: *I do not need to be anything other than myself, and I trust in my truth to radiate from that place of authenticity.*

It is no surprise that being the center of attention is something you crave with Mercury in the mighty sign of Leo; yet you provide substance behind the performance. Being gregarious and outgoing are among your best attributes, but what you say is more important than how you say it. Don't worry about your truth having to look good or serve some higher purpose; your own simple thoughts and feelings are always enough. Make sure that you do get to know your true self before entering into a relationship and that you allow your partner to see that part of you. You don't have to play the role of the perfect lover — just be yourself.

Sometimes your truth or meaning can get lost in how others see you. This disparity is neither their fault nor yours, but it is something to be aware of. Having a partner who allows you to embrace your uniqueness is important; you don't want someone who unintentionally boxes you into being only one way. Knowing that you need your partner's undivided attention when speaking or sharing intimate parts of your day, you may realize it's of benefit to ask if they have space to listen first. Your sensitivity to this will show compassion and understanding, which will in turn get you the same. It's all about articulating your needs instead of just assuming your partner should know them.

Most Complementary Mercury Placements: Aries, Virgo, and Pisces

Mercury in Virgo

Your Truth Lesson Affirmation: *I honor my truth and its ability to break apart illusions so that I live a life of harmony and security.*

With Mercury in detail-oriented Virgo, once you let go of feeling like every step of the way has to be perfectly planned out, you can recognize the benefit you might receive from your partner helping you to see things in a new way. Life will always feel more complicated than you planned for, but if you get caught up in trying to make everything perfect, you'll end up missing the greater purpose or meaning. You can see the minutiae in any situation but can become so focused on these little parts of life that you miss the bigger picture. Let go of the desire to control the outcome, and focus more on what is real. Instead of only seeing what isn't right, practice feeling gratitude for all that is.

Ask for your lover's perspective so that you might widen your view and let go of having to prove your ideas to anyone or needing your relationship to look a certain way. Having a partner who can hold space and talk things through with you is necessary, especially once you can be open to seeing that you might be able to learn from them. A partner who can challenge you to step out of your comfort zone creates more space for growth.

Most Complementary Mercury Placements: Taurus, Cancer, and Leo

Mercury in Libra

Your Truth Lesson Affirmation: *I will not sacrifice my inner peace at the expense of expressing my truth.*

You feel an innate sense of what is right and what is wrong when you have Mercury in Libra, aptly represented by the scales. You can become fixated on your inner sense of justice, which can prevent you from hearing your partner's opinions or beliefs, even if the two of you are not far apart in what you are expressing. Giving yourself time to learn that life isn't black and white but is, instead, made up of many colors can help you widen your perspective of what fairness consists of.

Making the effort to see things from their point of view and not just your own can make for a more balanced relationship. Try to understand that you do not have to be wrong for your partner to feel validated; instead of the pendulum swinging in one direction or the other, you want to find a middle ground together. Focus on your feelings, too, not just your thoughts, so that your authentic truth can shine through. There is no room to be a martyr for love; instead, it's about recognizing that keeping things to yourself can never create peace within yourself or in your relationship.

Most Complementary Mercury Placements: Sagittarius, Capricorn, and Aquarius

Mercury in Scorpio

Your Truth Lesson Affirmation: *I trust in my intuition to help me embrace my deepest emotions so that I can continually transform into my highest self.*

With Mercury in emotional Scorpio, your truth is more tied to what you feel than what you know. Feeling emotionally safe enough to share your deepest feelings with your partner is crucial to allow beneficial communication to flow. You could have a tendency toward judgment and keeping secrets, even if it comes from just not wanting to express your feelings out of fear of not having your needs met. Do not edit yourself for someone else's comfort. The more you become comfortable speaking your true feelings, the more likely you will attract someone who can listen and respond thoughtfully.

You have such great depth inside of you; feeling like no one can understand or appreciate it will only create a wall in your relationship. Allow your partner to see the real you and don't be afraid of having a need dismissed before you even ask. The "what if" game is something you tend to play when you go into overthinking mode; try to slow your brain and heart down and focus on the present moment. Being with a partner who can physically comfort you and hold space is just as important as their emotional capabilities.

Most Complementary Mercury Placements: Aries, Cancer, and Pisces

Mercury in Sagittarius

Your Truth Lesson Affirmation: *I embrace my truth as the pathway toward freedom so that I may live in alignment with my soul.*

So many possibilities exist for you with Mercury in Sagittarius, it can be overwhelming to pick the one you want to pursue. It is okay to talk things out with your partner without feeling like you must have everything figured out first; be each other's strength. Having a lover who is nonjudgmental and not controlling is incredibly important, so that you can feel free to express yourself before settling on one idea or truth as your own. Your partner should help guide you toward your own truth rather than forcing you to choose a particular direction. This means, though, that you need to be able to decipher what *is* your truth, or you can end up in a relationship that isn't aligned to your authentic self simply because you're able to see so many possibilities.

While being an explorer of life is part of your gift, you must first become certain of what you're seeking. Do not let life's distractions take you away from discovering your true self, and do not try to take on different personas to identify yourself. You don't need to be like your partner to make it work; only be yourself. You are your own person, and while you may have to follow a meandering path to your truth, it is always worth taking, because you do deserve to be loved in all the ways you desire.

Most Complementary Mercury Placements: Libra, Aquarius, and Pisces

Mercury in Capricorn

Your Truth Lesson Affirmation: *My truth is intrinsically connected to my purpose, and I will honor it and the changes that it brings to my life.*

With your Mercury in Capricorn, the bigger picture is something you must train yourself to see, as it can be easy to get lost in focusing on where you are now. And, while being able to envision your goal is important, you must also be aware that not all steps will lead to the same destination. Sometimes, to achieve a goal, you need to change direction altogether. Oftentimes, you tend to keep your head down and just keep following one path instead of reflecting on whether that path will lead to where you hope to be. This can play out in relationships by your focusing on the daily moments instead of considering whether a greater long-term alignment is present.

When you speak, be present in the moment; focus on where you want to see yourself with validation and authority. This intentionality will enable you to clearly communicate with your partner and help you put your own plan into action to accomplish a goal or handle a situation. It's necessary to have a partner who can trust your direction, even as they are able to provide a mirror for deeper reflection. For you, understanding that feelings are just as important as thoughts and actions is part of learning how to create a deeper love. You feel more fulfilled when you have accomplished what you set out to create; allowing your partner to be part of that process will help.

Most Complementary Mercury Placements: Taurus, Gemini, and Libra

Mercury in Aquarius

Your Truth Lesson Affirmation: *I honor my uniqueness and trust that in my soul I will always know what is best for me.*

Freedom to explore your ideas is the key to harnessing the magic behind your words when your Mercury is in far-seeing Aquarius. You see things differently than most, which means that you automatically tend to take the lead in conversations, including with your partner. You do not ever have to dumb yourself down, but you do have to be willing to let people come up with their own solutions, even if you can already see the outcome. Don't rob your partner of the lessons they need to learn for themselves. In love, you also need to learn there is no blueprint you follow.

While you may try early on to fulfill the stereotypical milestones of a relationship, you are happiest with a connection that defies any societal norms. This is truly the epitome of throwing out the rule book on love and coming up with what feels in alignment with your soul. You are a visionary in how you think about and process information. It is one of your greatest gifts; but following through is something you need to put equal energy into. Having a partner who allows you to talk things through and can help guide you toward that next logical step from time to time is essential. You have the ideas, but a partner who helps motivate you to make them real can make all the difference, especially if you're creating something unique together.

Most Complementary Mercury Placements: Gemini, Libra, and Sagittarius

Mercury in Pisces

Your Truth Lesson Affirmation: *My emotions are my truth, and they don't need to be explained, only embraced.*

Mercury in Pisces speaks from the soul, not the mind. This can lead you to feel isolated; you inherently see and feel things differently than most. You often must process your emotions before you share your thoughts for this very reason. You understand feelings on an intricate level and are a fantastic listener. Because you are so feeling based, having a partner who helps you process can be a vital addition to your life. They might offer this through thought-provoking questions or even challenging your beliefs. You also need someone who will match your heart's strength without making you feel as though your emotions do not matter. You'll know this is the case when you feel confident that they are just as passionate about life and invested in the relationship as you are.

There is no halfway in love, so making sure that you're not settling for less than the fullest love is an important part of honoring your truth. You have a gentle way of approaching others that invites them to share the deepest parts of themselves with you. Still, you must also utilize emotional boundaries so you do not take on their feelings in an empathetic way. You are not responsible for fixing your partner or the emotions they feel. Learning to speak your emotional truth without needing the validation of others opens up a new type of relating in love.

Most Complementary Mercury Placements: Leo, Scorpio, and Sagittarius

Soulmate Relationships Charts
and Journal Prompts

Fill in the blank charts below to create the birth charts for yourself, your partner, and your familial relationships. If you'd like additional blank charts, you can also download them at WordsOfKateRose.com.

NAME:	
Sun	
Moon	
Mercury	
Venus	
Mars	
Jupiter	
Saturn	
Uranus	
Neptune	
Pluto	
North Node	
South Node	
Rising	

NAME:	
Sun	
Moon	
Mercury	
Venus	
Mars	
Jupiter	
Saturn	
Uranus	
Neptune	
Pluto	
North Node	
South Node	
Rising	

NAME:	
Sun	
Moon	
Mercury	
Venus	
Mars	
Jupiter	
Saturn	
Uranus	
Neptune	
Pluto	
North Node	
South Node	
Rising	

NAME:	
Sun	
Moon	
Mercury	
Venus	
Mars	
Jupiter	
Saturn	
Uranus	
Neptune	
Pluto	
North Node	
South Node	
Rising	

Being Honest with Yourself Is the First Step

While you are contemplating the astrology charts for you and your partner, it will be helpful to reflect on some critical questions that will lead to the answers you are seeking.

What do you notice is similar between your charts? Do you both share the same Saturn sign, or is there a strong repetition of each other's Saturn sign in other placements?

What differences exist, especially between the sun, Venus, moon, and Mercury or Mars placements?

Can you see a pattern of where you choose on the basis of sameness rather than of complementary energy?

Knowing that the sun, Venus, moon, Mercury, and Mars represent your emotional intelligence, love language, emotional vulnerability, communication, and passion, respectively, do you feel any of these areas as challenging in the relationship?

This is also the place where you can compare your chart with the astrology charts for your parents and/or caregivers to see if a pattern from childhood is emerging. For instance, a client has her Saturn in the same sign as both her parents' Venus, indicating she likely didn't feel loved in the ways that she needed. She then goes on to attract a partner with that same zodiac sign in multiple placements, signifying that she has an ongoing pattern that will only become undone when she learns to love herself.

While the childhood patterns in astrology usually come out later, in karmic and twin flame relationships, you might even notice an important theme that is beginning to play out in your romantic life in the soulmate relationship.

If the partner you thought was a forever love is starting to look, instead, like a soulmate, ask yourself what part your authentic truth plays in the connection. Use the lesson of the truth affirmation from the Mercury section earlier to decipher if this is something you are actively practicing in your current relationship or not.

Authenticity is one of the most important factors for determining if your relationship is serving as a hiding place from having to speak your truth or a haven encouraging you to do just that.

Are you aware of your truth?

If you are, then what is preventing you from living it?

If not, what are you afraid of discovering if you do?

Look to your childhood, your experiences, and how you were loved. Did you feel validated? Were you taught to trust yourself? If not, then you may need to go back so that you can feel freer to go forward. It's common during this time to start to become aware of the childhood wounds that you might be guided to bring healing to.

It is always scary to grow and be unsure of the outcome of your decisions, yet no one is ever 100 percent sure of anything new before they do it. It all comes down to the trust that you have within yourself.

For any new decisions, especially one to end a relationship, you are only aiming to be about 70 percent sure, because there will always be doubts and there will always be fear around doing something new.

Your brain is conditioned to keep you safe, yet this only ever translates into things staying the same. Even though you could be on the brink of a moment of huge growth, your brain could resist simply because it doesn't register the growth as being safe. When you can validate your own feelings and find a sense of safety within yourself, you will be more apt to accept the risk, to trust in the 70 percent certainty, and not to let anything hold you back from this brand-new chapter in your life.

Remember: nothing ever truly ends — it just transforms into something different.

Affirmations for the Soulmate Relationship

I trust myself and my heart to always know what is right for me.
I am allowed to grow out of the person that I was.
Life is always changing, but I do not need to fear the changes life brings.
The love that is meant for me will always be able to receive and accept my truth.
I am worthy of being loved for who I am.
I deserve to live the life and be the person I dream of.
I can acknowledge that while I love my family, I know in my heart I need to make decisions that are for my highest good.
It is up to me to heal the generational wounds that are keeping me from living my truth.
I can create the life of my dreams and uphold the responsibilities I value.
I do not need to choose between freedom and roots, because I carry both within me.
Only I hold the power to change my life, which means it is only my inner self I listen to.
I choose peace and affirm it is more important than fear.
I understand that there is no perfect time for me to make changes in my life, and I will work on healing myself so that I do not procrastinate on the creation of my dreams.
I am loved and I am worthy to be loved by someone who enables me to embrace my truth.

Moon Rituals for the Soulmate Relationship

The phases of the moon have long been revered for their healing powers. Ancient cultures recognized that each moon phase held significance for the growing season of their crops or the birthing season of the animals. The moon's phases represented a time to rest, plant new beginnings, or reap the harvest of what was sown.

The moon's journey through our sky is a language of cycles passed down for generations to help you recognize the passing of time, not by a clock, but by the natural world around you. It holds the promise of what is to come while also acknowledging the importance of what no longer is.

The most crucial aspect of the soulmate relationship is letting go. But I don't necessarily mean letting go of the connection altogether, as it often transforms into one between friends, coparents, or simply family. Instead, it is about letting go of your attachment to it.

It is understanding that you needed this relationship to define who you were at a certain point, because you had not yet learned that defining who you were was something you had to do for yourself. Releasing the soulmate relationship is letting go of the sense of validation it may have brought to your life as you fulfilled the social or familial expectations of what is "right" or what you "should" be doing.

Letting go of your attachment to it means that you do not lose anything by allowing the relationship to transform into something different: now, you can fill your own cup and satisfy the empty parts of yourself.

You no longer need this relationship to define you, because you have learned how to do that for yourself. All that is left for you to do is to let go and prepare to receive what the universe has in store for you.

Full-Moon Release Ritual

Healing Crystals

Labradorite: This is a protection stone that can help you open to receive divine messages from the universe and let go of attachments to old ways of thinking.

Onyx: This is an essential stone for boundaries: it will keep you from taking on the feelings of those around you as your own. Not everyone will approve of your decisions in life, but this stone can help strengthen you.

Rhodonite: Being afraid of your new path is expected. This crystal can bring calmness to your nervous system so that you do not let a momentary feeling disrupt the path your soul knows it should pursue.

How to Perform the Full-Moon Ritual of Release

Under the full moon of your choosing, write a letter to your past self. While you can perform this during any full moon, it will have added intensity if you can do it during your own moon sign or a full moon that occurs as part of an eclipse.

In this letter, write down all you have learned from your soulmate relationship while expressing gratitude for your partner's role and your ability to move through the lessons.

Most importantly, write down the forgiveness you have for yourself for those choices you made when you did not know better, for staying in a comfort zone far longer than you now see you needed to, and for being called in a different direction than you had anticipated.

As you near the end of your letter, release yourself from this relationship. Release your attachment to the validation it provided, the conditioning you thought you had to uphold, and the fear that you are somehow making a mistake by following your soul.

Once you have finished writing your letter, fold it three times, bring it and your crystals outside under the light of the full moon, and place the letter in a container or space where it is safe to burn it. Light the letter on fire while repeating the soulmate affirmations that call to you.

When the ashes have cooled, bury them in your garden with rosemary and/or cedar and lay the crystals on top. You will leave them there for a full lunar cycle.

Place your hands on your heart and allow yourself to cry if you feel called to. Cry for the ending, the transformation, and most of all for the love that you still have for this person.

But through it all, keep your hands on your heart as you choose the path of your soul. The one that you know is leading you in a new and vibrant direction.

Part Two

THE ASTROLOGY OF
KARMIC RELATIONSHIPS

It feels like I should invite you to take a deep breath before you begin this section, and you may even have exhaled when you turned the page.

Karmic relationships are truly the stuff of legends.

It was once common to believe that your karmic relationship was your twin flame, simply because of the intensity of feelings that were present. However, while the twin flame relationship heals, the karmic destroys. There is no other way.

It is brutal, passionate, electrifying. And yet nothing will bring you to your knees more deeply than your karmic connection. This relationship is truly an experience of entering the flames so that you can eventually rise as the phoenix.

Your karmic connection can come at any time. While most experience their soulmate relationship first, if you've had a more traumatic childhood or your inner teenager is more prominent, your karmic connection could be the first one you attract. If it is, you could potentially stay within this cycle until you finally learn the purpose of it. Just as the soulmate relationship is more indicative of your childlike perception of life and love, your karmic connection tends to be more representative of your inner teenager. This is why so many of these relationships tend to involve third parties: the karmic connection often comes into the picture once you are married or in a heavily committed relationship and have begun to reflect on your desire to rebel against the status quo.

The karmic relationship is the space of learning, growing, and maturing into a conscious adult, so that you not only speak your truth but also honor your needs and embrace healthier ways of relating in love. Your karmic relationship is what applies exactly enough pressure so you can see, for the first time, your own worth. It becomes not just an important lesson but the moment when everything changes.

While you had to leave your soulmate relationship to grow, in your karmic connection you are faced with the decision of choosing your healing over your wounds. You have to embody everything you were ever looking for in another and know, with complete confidence, that you were never asking for too much.

You were just asking for it from a person who could never give it to you.

Your Hurts Will Lead to Healing

While your soulmate relationship was comfortable, your karmic connection is anything but — yet it doesn't matter, because you won't be able to stay away. The safety and peace you felt in your soulmate relationship doesn't exist in your karmic connection.

It's one that induces anxiety, has you reflecting on your attachment style, and makes you feel very unsure about where it's all headed. In fact, the inconsistency is the only consistency. Within your soulmate connection, the soul lesson was to become aware of your truth, of your own authentic self, and to start to live from this newly found space. It created a separation, not necessarily because anything was terribly wrong or bad, but simply because you'd outgrown the life perspective and validation that the relationship provided you.

As you're transitioning out of your soulmate relationship — that childhood-like phase of wanting to be safe, secure, and accepted — you'll enter your karmic phase, or the one more like your rebellious teen years (even if you never got to embrace that resistance while growing up).

These relationships mirror the lessons of love that you move through, and which relationship you're in depends on where you are with yourself. So the soulmate relationship mirrors your childhood self, your karmic relationship reflects those tempestuous teen years, and the twin flame connection shows us the adult, conscious, secure, ever-healing self.

One is not better than the others. None is perfect. Think of them more as a progression.

As you progress through your own journey of awareness, you naturally move into various stages within your romantic life. But nothing is like the karmic connection. In it you are tasked with learning about and healing the wounds that you've come into this life with, as well as those that you have experienced since birth.

If there was a history of people-pleasing or scarcity mindset within your lineage, your karmic relationship is where you'll be invited to participate in generational healing. If you didn't feel unconditionally loved as a child, this is the relationship that will encourage self-love. If you lacked boundaries or self-validation, then this is the relationship that will make the necessity of those apparent.

But the thing is, there will also be great love.

You will project everything you are and everything you have ever wanted onto another person. It will feel as if they are your air, your purpose, and your sole reason for being incarnated in this life. And this is why the karmic connection offers the most difficult lesson: because it's a love that feels addicting. There is no point in trying to say otherwise, because it just isn't the truth.

The karmic relationship doesn't just come in and out of your life within a few months. You will usually spend years or even decades enmeshed within it, feeling at times that you simply can't get out. Even though many view this as wasted time, it isn't. Even if, as you're reading this now, tears begin to fall on these pages, know that not a moment is ever wasted in a karmic relationship. If you have been in one, you have gone through precisely what you were meant to go through and in the exact time frame that you were meant to do so.

After your soulmate lesson, you are ripe with the bud of truth — yet you are just beginning to explore what this means for you and your life. You are looking for love to be more exciting, to give you thrills, and to seem like the greatest love story ever told, so that you can feel validated in having ended your soulmate relationship.

To know that yes, it was worth it.

And so you attract exactly what you need in order to learn about your own wounds, to start identifying what hurts or what beliefs are directing your thoughts and actions. You start to address your own stuff and begin to understand the significance of balance, because while your soulmate relationship was secure, your karmic is anything but.

It all serves a purpose.

You need to go from one extreme to another to figure out that you don't have to choose between consistency and passion, excitement and stability, or the various parts of your own self. Because while each relationship is indicative of a different part of yourself, none of the parts ever go away.

There will never be a time that your inner child doesn't deserve to be loved in all the ways you've ever desired. There is never a moment that your inner teenager won't need the freedom to explore and grow. And there is also never a time when your healing adult self can't integrate that all into one relationship. Yet to learn those lessons and have the confidence to practice them, you need to be right here, in this moment of trying to learn if your relationship is indeed karmic or else processing it because you're already certain.

You need to just be wherever you are to get where you want to be; there is no rush, because this step is just as important as the next.

And that means it's also time to open the vault of your heart, to look at your wounds, to excavate the beliefs you were raised with and the generational trauma that has been handed down to you. While you didn't ask to take on your healing and that of your ancestors, you are being called to participate in it because you are meant to be the one who changes everything.

Not just for yourself or for your romantic life, but for the collective.

To grow isn't only to move on, but to heal your roots so they don't stop you or future generations from flourishing — from eventually reaching not just the moon, but the sun too.

The Lessons of the South Node

One of the most common questions I receive is "How do I know if a relationship is karmic or if it's something else?" Part of the answer, of course, comes down to actually trusting your own self without needing the external validation of "proof." That said, in my time with clients, I did start to recognize and develop a way to determine if a relationship is genuinely karmic.

The patterning in the charts of a karmic connection is completely different from what you'll find if you look up astrological compatibility, yet it's one that has never been wrong in all of the work that I've done with clients around the world. And it's simple: it is based on what your karmic lessons are.

The lessons of your karmic relationship are not just about love or relationships, but about your being able to set yourself free from everything that was never really a part of your truth to begin with. Your karmic relationship is one that changes the entire course of your life; there is forever a before and an after that reverberate throughout your existence. Your karmic lesson shows up in two ways in your astrology chart: the first is in your South Node, and the second is in the patterns that emerge in the charts of your parents and romantic partners.

The North and South Nodes are simply mathematical points that describe the relationship between the sun, moon, and earth at the time of your birth. Each one represents a particular set of elements.

The South Node represents the karma that you were born into this life with, that which you are meant to move through in this lifetime. This is also the place where karma you have carried over from past lifetimes exists. Generational, past-life, and childhood-wound karma are often present in these types of relationships and are another clue identifying the relationship you are in as one meant to teach you an important lesson.

But there can be many factors at play within the karmic relationship. For example, you and your partner could have the same South Node, their Saturn sign may be the same as your South Node, or your romantic partner might have the same Venus sign as your father. The union in which partners share the same South Node represents not just your own personal lessons but also generational wounds or conditioning that you experienced as a child. There are also relationships that might offer a karmic lesson for you, but not for your partner. These often are the most challenging because your partner won't understand your experience of the relationship, as the purpose of it for them will be vastly different than the one for yourself and healing journey.

To gain greater clarity on your karmic relationship, refer to your parents' Saturn and South Node signs, then compare them to your partner's Saturn, South Node, sun, and Venus signs. If you see a repetition of zodiac signs — for example, if your partner has the same Saturn sign as one of your parents — it means this relationship holds an important lesson for each of you. If the pattern is only present for you — for example, if your Venus sign is the same as your parent's South Node — it means it's just your lesson to learn. And if only your partner has those connections, it means the relationship carries a karmic lesson only for them. While having the same Saturn sign as your partner denotes the karma in a soulmate connection, this similarity may also hold clues to continuing to heal through your karmic relationship, especially as you start to compare the birth charts of your parents. This is because often if you hadn't yet unpacked your childhood wounding or trauma, you will attract a partner that will allow you to do just that.

A karmic relationship tends to last a significant period of time because the lessons that you're moving through aren't just yours, but those that have been handed down to you through different generations and your own lifetimes. Your karmic lesson is never all bad; if it were, it would be easy to leave. Instead, the karmic relationship has just enough of what your inner child or teenager has always longed for — just enough possibility and often just enough hope — to keep you hooked for years, until you finally learn that no matter what you do, it doesn't actually get better, and that you deserve more than just the breadcrumbs of an amazing love.

The Lesson Is the Blessing

No one wants to hear that the relationship they've thought was their great love is actually just a lesson, but knowledge is freedom — the freedom to choose differently. And nothing is solely a lesson; you will be shaped by the experiences you have while together and by how much you are able to grow.

To ultimately learn your karmic lesson, you will enter into a relationship with someone whose chart has similarities with your South Node or will represent a larger pattern that is connected to the astrology of your parents. These astrological aspects provide a crucial mirroring effect. You often can't see what you need to do to grow or change until you're faced with it right in front of you.

Even if in this moment, as you are reading, something is tugging at your soul telling you that the relationship you've believed was your divine love might be your karmic, you should not transition out of it just because I, another book, or a beloved friend told you to. That decision has to come out of the lessons that you've learned. If you do leave because of the voice of another, what I always see is that you will attract another similar relationship, because you still have to learn the lesson you are meant to.

Let me tell you about Julia, a client who reached out for clarity around her relationship.

When Julia was young, she was in an unhealthy marriage. Issues of control and emotional abuse were present, along with a toxic cycle of love bombing and wounding. Julia's parents stepped in and told her that she needed to end her marriage, or she would be cut out of the family business. They even went so far as to move her husband out of the house.

On some level Julia knew she had to leave the relationship, but she hadn't reached that point yet for herself, and she did it solely because she was forced to by her parents. Her family, of course, couldn't help but want to save her, but in doing so, they only prolonged the time her karmic lesson would take.

After ending her marriage, Julia was in and out of dating relationships, never really having a significant partner and actually spending a good portion of time alone while she continued to raise her children.

Until one day she crossed paths with a new man, Elijah.

At first Elijah seemed to be too good to be true. He was a hotel owner, loving and affectionate, and seemed to exude the zest for life that Julia craved. However, as time progressed, she began to doubt her own experiences of the relationship. Elijah tried to convince Julia of the version of himself that he wanted to be seen as instead of the truth of who he actually was. It was because of this relationship that Julia reached out to me for help. Immediately, I could sense that Elijah was engaging in some gaslighting. Ultimately, Julia had to get to the place where she was making her own choices for the relationship on the basis of her experience. She had to find her voice, validate her own decisions, and glean what actually felt like truth to her — regardless of what anyone else said or tried to make her believe. Of course, the relationship with Elijah lasted longer than it would have if she'd listened to outside advice, and it had to become worse before she could finally make the choice for the better — but she did.

One of the factors that we spoke about in great detail was the similarities between her relationship with Elijah and her first marriage, which her parents forced her to end. She could see how, although her parents were only doing what they thought was right, she had attracted Elijah so that she could learn the karmic lessons she had missed when her first marriage ended too soon: what her own worth was in a relationship and how to advocate for herself.

JULIA	
Sun	Cancer
Moon	Libra
Mercury	Scorpio
Venus	Aquarius
Mars	Aries
Jupiter	Sagittarius
Saturn	Sagittarius
Uranus	Leo
Neptune	Scorpio
Pluto	Virgo
North Node	Leo
South Node	Aquarius
Rising	Cancer

ELIJAH	
Sun	Aquarius
Moon	Cancer
Mercury	Capricorn
Venus	Gemini
Mars	Leo
Jupiter	Sagittarius
Saturn	Sagittarius
Uranus	Leo
Neptune	Scorpio
Pluto	Virgo
North Node	Pisces
South Node	Virgo
Rising	Aquarius

No one can ever rescue you from your karmic relationship, no matter how deeply friends or family may love you, because you have to learn that the only person who can save you is yourself. When you allow others to lead the choices in your life, you aren't stepping into your own power, and therefore you are not being your authentic self. You are merely letting others direct your life. Instead, you need to learn that only you will know what is right for you.

In looking at the charts of Julia and Elijah, you will also see that Julia's South Node is the same as Elijah's sun and rising signs. This means that in this partnership, she's moving not just through her own present-life lessons but through those that she came into this life with.

With the strong connection between her South Node and his astrology chart, I advised her to go slowly, to proceed with awareness and caution, because it represented the hallmarks of the true karmic relationship, and there would be an important lesson for her to learn and clearing for her to do. In this situation, the couple's charts denoted that the relationship really wasn't healthy for either of them, even if Elijah was the only one displaying significant toxic behaviors.

As wonderfully awful as this type of union is, it's also clearer than the relationship where someone is your lesson but you are not theirs. Let's turn to Michael and Steven.

Michael reached out to me because he was having concerns over his romantic relationship. He wasn't sure if Steven was being faithful, and it seemed that no matter what he tried, how he grew, or how much patience he practiced, the relationship never got better.

In comparing their two charts (shown on the next page), you will notice that their Saturn signs are different, so you might think that this is a healthy, long-lasting relationship. However, the South Node tells a different story. Michael's South Node was unconsciously attracted to Steven's sun sign because it would give him the opportunity to work through healing the wounds that he came into this life with, some of which are his from previous lifetimes and others of which have been passed on through generations.

MICHAEL	
Sun	Leo
Moon	Pisces
Mercury	Cancer
Venus	Aries
Mars	Capricorn
Jupiter	Sagittarius
Saturn	Libra
Uranus	Scorpio
Neptune	Sagittarius
Pluto	Libra
North Node	Pisces
South Node	Virgo
Rising	Capricorn

STEVEN	
Sun	Virgo
Moon	Aries
Mercury	Scorpio
Venus	Gemini
Mars	Taurus
Jupiter	Leo
Saturn	Virgo
Uranus	Scorpio
Neptune	Sagittarius
Pluto	Libra
North Node	Cancer
South Node	Capricorn
Rising	Libra

There isn't horrible alignment here, which is usually the case in karmic connections — the charts won't look like the worst possible combination — but there is an underlying energy through Saturn and the South Node signifying that the main purpose of the relationship is the lesson that Michael needs to learn.

In this case, Steven also has Venus in Gemini, one of the more challenging placements for the planet of love, as it often suggests that someone will have difficulty in committing or being faithful. It is the astrological marker of having a wandering eye and is frequently present in the charts of those who have had multiple affairs or simply are unable to make a definitive choice in their romantic life.

As Michael and I talked about the charts, we started to pick apart the relationship he had with Steven and examine what he felt he was continually being called on to deal with. One of the major realizations Michael had was that he felt he always had to compromise his needs in order to keep Steven in his life. Whatever Steven didn't want to do, he didn't; and Michael was left to either accept it or to finally move on toward what he genuinely deserved. This is a typical dynamic in relationships that hold a karmic lesson for only one partner; as far as Steven was concerned, everything was fine. Michael was meeting Steven's needs, he was there when he wanted him to be, and he was able to live his life however he desired. It was Michael who felt like he was continually having to make allowances, swallow his own truth, or settle for what was being offered in order to remain in the relationship.

Sometimes this disjunction comes up in connections in which one person feels more of a soulmate dynamic but the other is moving through karmic lessons; this can be the reality. Just because someone is your soulmate doesn't mean that you're not their karmic partner. The only connection that will exclusively show up in the same way for you both is your twin flame, your divine love.

But regardless of the form the karmic relationship takes, you must understand that your lesson will always be revealed to you in the ways that you need it to be. You didn't ask for this type of relationship — for the confusion, the hurt, and the guilt as you try to make it work — but it is still your responsibility to move through it so that you can embrace your own healing and authenticity.

I've been asked before, "Can a karmic relationship be saved if both people learn their lessons?"

Of course, no one wants to think of having to separate from

someone they love. And in many ways, keeping the relationship going beyond the lessons learned could make sense, because in any relationship there has to be ongoing growth, healing, and forgiveness. But the defining factor in a karmic connection is that even if you and your partner both learn your karmic lessons and dive into the healing of your inner children, you won't be able to transition into a healthy, stable love, let alone a twin flame, divine love relationship.

Without question, your karmic relationship is special, it's unique, and it helps you become the person you are meant to evolve into. However, no matter how much you learn, how much you heal your anxious attachment, or how much you practice advocating for yourself, compromising, or giving second chances, this connection will only ever end up the same way, because it's not actually meant to become more. This was your path at birth, long before you met your partner. And sometimes having a relationship written in the stars means that it was also always meant to end.

You will be asked to sacrifice your own growth for the ability to continue with the relationship or to choose yourself, validate your own truth, and have faith that the love you seek does exist — you just haven't been in the place to attract it yet. As a firm believer in the possibility of growth for everyone, I can say with conviction that it is never too late to learn.

Because all it takes is one moment — one moment of clarity, of honesty, of blazing self-worth — for you to realize that you deserve more. And that is also the very moment you begin attracting it.

Understanding Your South Node

To embrace the growth that your South Node represents, you first have to understand the lessons it carries. This is done by learning what the karmic lesson is according to your zodiac sign.

The South Node works in similar ways to Saturn in your soulmate relationship, but it carries with it the awareness that the lessons you are moving through aren't just yours from this lifetime. They are also those you came into this life with or those handed down to you from your ancestors for healing.

Your karmic lesson isn't a burden to carry, but a gift, because while learning it may not be easy, it holds the key to transforming yourself, your romantic relationship, and your entire life. By learning your karmic lesson, you unlock your fate. You no longer work against yourself while trying to create the life of your dreams, but finally are in the place to cocreate it with the universe.

Your Zodiac Karmic Lessons

The South Node in Aries

Your Karmic Lesson Affirmation: *I am able to be myself and still create a relationship of balance.*

The karmic lesson of having the South Node in Aries means that you likely are overly independent. You struggle to rely on someone, to embrace help, or to entertain the possibility that another might see a better way than you. In this dynamic, you will tend to attract a partner who is codependent or extremely needy and is desperate for what you are able to provide them. Or, conversely, you may end up in a relationship with someone who is trying to control you. You often have to swing between two extremes to find the lesson of balance.

The South Node in Aries is used to taking care of things on their own, so in this relationship it could be that you have to take care of everything — or, again conversely, it could be that someone is trying to do that for you but robbing you of your autonomy in exchange for validating your inner child. Be mindful of becoming a martyr for love or of letting your sense of responsibility be the sole basis for the choices you make. As foreign as it might feel, it's not your job to solve the problems of your partner or the world in order to deserve love.

You don't have to trade freedom for love or authenticity in order to receive affection. You deserve the balance of having someone there to help you, someone who has their own amazing life while you get to do the same. The more that you can recognize the areas where you feel exhausted by others, the more you can take back that energy and reinvest it in yourself. You can't keep doing for others or allow resentment to build inside because of the controlling personality of another.

The South Node in Aries helps you deal with your feelings of abandonment or feeling that no one was ever there to help you. As you learn better boundaries, prioritize your own self, and realize that you don't need to save others the way you wish someone had saved you, you'll also start to recognize that you truly do deserve a healthy love.

The South Node in Taurus

Your Karmic Lesson Affirmation: *I am able to keep myself safe and deserve to receive the love that I desire.*

You can't trade your own truth for security, no matter how many times you try. With the South Node in Taurus, you tend to want things to be very stable, grounded, and straightforward; you prioritize sameness over having a healthy, balanced relationship. Reflect on how you have chosen the stability of your relationship over having the love you yearn for. Just because someone may wake up next to you each morning doesn't mean that it's the relationship you truly desire. You can look for what is consistent, but if it still ends up lacking alignment or you have to water down parts of yourself in order to keep it afloat, then it's not a healthy relationship.

Oftentimes you will attract one of two extremes: either a relationship you feel you can't escape from because of the obligations that exist or a partner who is incredibly unsettled within themselves. In these cases, your karmic lesson will be that no matter how much you equate stability with things remaining the same, if the relationship lacks the principles of healthy love, all you are left with is not feeling seen or heard. Someone loving you on paper is different from someone loving the essence of who you really are.

On the flip side, as someone who craves consistency and stability, you may attract a karmic partner who has addiction or commitment issues. You will struggle to keep the relationship together while having to learn that you can't fix someone else.

Ultimately, the lesson for you is to redirect your quest for stability and safety toward your own self. As you recognize that you can keep yourself safe and remain stable regardless of what changes around you, you will be less and less apt to stay in relationships that don't actually promote that. And when you learn that you are your own safe space, suddenly, creating that outside of yourself becomes the easiest thing in the world to do.

The South Node in Gemini

Your Karmic Lesson Affirmation: *I am embracing my own truth in order to take accountability and action in creating a healthy relationship.*

There is power in duality, but only once you learn how to embrace it for your highest good. People with the South Node in Gemini frequently come across as having very scattered energy. You might say, for example, that you want a committed, long-lasting relationship, yet your actions or choices send a different message. You might choose a partner who genuinely is a healthy match, yet still keep that uncommitted ex on the side just in case.

You often crave excitement from love, which you find through having multiple partners, through infidelity, or by thrilling in doing something that you know ultimately doesn't align with your truth. You also tend to put new partners on a higher pedestal than any previous ones. This romanticized story you create with new partners centers on the belief that if you are with the right person, then you would finally receive the validation you've been in search of.

But this isn't the case.

You will tend to attract the emotionally unavailable, uncommitted, or downright player-type energy. Or you may go to the opposite extreme: your partner may be more of an introverted homebody, while you want to go out and have fun and party with friends on the weekend.

For you to start to embody the truth of your karmic lesson, you have to be accountable for what you bring to the relationship. Start to look at your own emotional availability and the fears you may hold around being vulnerable and getting rejected. It's easier to think the challenges you face are everyone else's fault, but at some point, you have to decide who you authentically are so that you can build a life from that.

However, Gemini energy rules your ego as well as your soul, and there's power in that. And while Gemini's tendency to swing between two extremes may be confusing while you're on the journey of learning your lesson — after all, your soul might say love, but your ego craves a fleeting vacation tryst — this is the place of opportunity for you. Your ego isn't bad, so long as it's grounded in the truth of your soul. As you look at why you are attracting the people you are in relationship with and at your own level of accountability within the relationship, then you will progress to the place where you will choose your own destiny — and healing.

The South Node in Cancer

Your Karmic Lesson Affirmation: *I am worthy of prioritizing my own happiness above all others.*

The South Node in Cancer always holds one of the most difficult lessons, because it ties into family themes. It is said that these are the ties that bind, and in this case it's often binding you to trauma and wounding. During your karmic relationship, it will feel like either you can't leave the family you've created or you have to do whatever it takes to please the family you were raised by. Possibly even both.

Maintaining a family structure this way, though, is at the cost of your self and your truth. This realization is ultimately what will come to the surface, because no matter how you might convince yourself otherwise, you can't force yourself to be happy with something that isn't meant to be.

Emotional manipulation, gaslighting, and financial control will likely be elements in this karmic relationship, as well as keeping secrets. You will feel that if you leave the relationship, you will lose everything that you value. Oftentimes it's not unheard of that children, biological or otherwise, factor heavily into the karmic relationship. But in having to face your own fear of abandonment and the possibility of being rejected by the family unit, you are facing the parts of yourself that have been lying in wait.

No matter how much you may love your family, you can't make decisions based on their happiness. You can't make the choices that give you their approval if inside you are rejecting your own truth. Being able to self-validate becomes incredibly important in this karmic connection, as you will need to build up your own sense of self in order to be able to transition out of this stage of life.

The more that you can discover what defines you and where your own worth is centered, the more you will be able to make the decisions necessary for a healthy love — no matter how challenging it might seem.

The South Node in Leo

Your Karmic Lesson Affirmation: *I am enough as I am and am deserving of attracting a true partner.*

Ego is healthy to have, as it helps you to understand what you are worth and allows you to set boundaries to protect you from what isn't meant for you. However, too much of anything — including ego — creates an entirely new obstacle that needs to be overcome.

With the South Node in Leo, you are often in battle with your ego, even if it feels like the battles have to do with your partner. It can frequently seem like you are being let down, like no matter what you do or try, you are never able to have your needs met.

The issue may also be that you're choosing someone who looks like the perfect partner for you, whether through physicality, career, or background — but they aren't. This can happen because your ego is trying to choose what it thinks will reflect back positively on you, meaning that if your partner is attractive, is financially stable, or is generating the spiritual energy of the enlightened, then you will be seen that way as well.

When you overcompensate by trying to have your relationship give you the validation that you haven't yet discovered is already within you, you are operating from a lack of self-confidence and inner worthiness. During your karmic relationship, when you feel like you've tried everything to make it work, you will be ready to move through the process of no longer villainizing your partner and instead reflect more deeply on what it was you were receiving from the connection itself.

This then becomes the blueprint showing you what to cultivate within yourself so that you can heal. Your lesson is to understand that others can't make up for the sense of lack within you — only you can do that.

The South Node in Virgo

Your Karmic Lesson Affirmation: *I am not perfect, but I am capable of giving myself all that I need.*

Many paths can lead to the same destination, but for those with the South Node in Virgo, it's a lesson to be learned. You tend to be very stuck in what you think is right, how you think things should be, and — whether you say it or not — the belief that your way is the right way.

Usually, you will attract someone who eventually refuses to play by your rules. They will challenge you with inconsistent behavior, an avoidant attachment style, and likely even some unfaithfulness. Yet you will remain determined that if only they would do things your way or whatever way you think is right, then all of this could be fixed. Of course, one of your major lessons is learning not to be codependent, as no matter how much energy you pour into someone else or the relationship, you can't ultimately determine what the relationship is meant to become.

You are one of the healers of the zodiac, but because of that, you often pick projects instead of partners. Reflect on your need to be of service or value to others instead of being with someone who challenges you to compromise, embrace flexibility, and focus on your own self-care. Likely in this lesson you will be asked to abandon yourself for the sake of another. You might pour all your energy into trying to help your partner create a career, make a big life change, or become the person that they're meant to be. As you step into the role of parent or caregiver, this creates an unbalanced dynamic; the relationship becomes less about what you need and more about what they do.

As you move through this karmic lesson, it's important to recognize the difference between helping and enabling and to prioritize yourself, your needs, your growth, and your care over anything else. In a truly healthy relationship, you won't have to abandon your dreams or financial security to raise up your partner or pour so much energy into them that you have none left for yourself.

Return to yourself and recognize that if you actually want a partner, you have to give them the space to genuinely show up as one.

The South Node in Libra

Your Karmic Lesson Affirmation: *I am no longer keeping the peace outside of myself at the expense of my own feelings.*

With your South Node in Libra, you harness all the justice and peace-keeping skills of the zodiac, However, in your karmic relationship, you end up focusing on what you're doing externally instead of what you're giving to yourself. You will be sacrificing your own internal peace and truth for the benefit of others, often being in relationship with some-one who goes against everything that your moral compass points to.

You will be asked to entertain new relationship paradigms — such as "living apart together," polyamory, or a situationship, which lacks the clarity and commitment of a defined relationship — and you will stay, at least for a significant period of time. Under the energy of the South Node in Libra, you have to work through your fear of starting arguments or of being abandoned, which causes you to remain si-lent, as you develop your own internal sense of truth. You often try to people-please your way through life as you prioritize their hurts, their growth, and their struggles ahead of your own. The result is that you completely abandon *yourself* to hang onto a relationship that isn't even providing you with what you need.

During this process, advocating for yourself becomes hugely important, as does being able to articulate when you are upset or angry. You don't need to always have a rational explanation for how you feel, nor do you have to keep cool all of the time. Anger is a normal and healthy emotion, and as long as you are doing your own reflective work to figure out why you feel that way, then it serves a purpose. The more that you can advocate for yourself, speak your truth, and release the ideas that love will ask you for silence and require you to become a doormat for your partner's unhealthy behaviors, the stronger you will grow, until you can finally transition out of this relationship and realize that the greatest peace can be found within yourself.

The South Node in Scorpio

Your Karmic Lesson Affirmation: *I am worthy of both passion and commitment, and I release any failure associated with the ending of a relationship.*

Scorpio is known as one of the deepest water signs — in fact, this sign has no problem doing the dirty work of life in order to achieve its deepest desires. With your South Node in this sign, however, you will reach a point in your karmic relationship where you have to understand that no matter how hard you work, it doesn't guarantee success, and you can't save another.

You are able to entertain more of the darkness of life than most other signs. Because of this, you tend to attract dark partners who will tempt you with the depth that is associated with addiction, abuse, or oversexualized behaviors. One of the lessons of this connection is that you can't use sex as a Band-Aid for what can't be fixed. But this lesson also leads you to recognize and validate your deep desire for commitment alongside passion. It will only feel like you have to choose between the two when you still are doubting that it is possible to have both.

Many times in this karmic connection, the relentless effort of trying to make a relationship work prevents you from having your emotional needs fulfilled, which is what fuels the oversexualized behavior. Sex might feel like the only way that you can feel connected to your partner, but rarely is sex all that you want. Nonetheless, even if they don't show up for you emotionally or supportively, you still will seek out intimacy to fill that void. Yet over time you will start to realize that the cycle actually depletes you. This is because, while sex is an amazing human experience, if you are letting someone who isn't honoring your divine worth have access to the best parts of you, then you're also participating in your own wounding.

You will find salve for your heart and be able to finally move on when you learn to establish healthy boundaries, honor yourself first, and recognize that no matter how badly you want a relationship to work, it may not be meant to be.

The South Node in Sagittarius

Your Karmic Lesson Affirmation: *I am able to be free and deserve to be loved for exactly the person who I am.*

The only way that you can learn to be free is by first being restricted. It seems unbelievable that a person with their South Node in Sagittarius, a sign that craves freedom, exploration, and knowledge, will enter into a relationship where these very things are unavailable — yet that is precisely what you need to experience so that you can set your own self free.

The placement of the South Node in Sagittarius is all about movement and new horizons, yet there is a part of you that questions your own worthiness or ability to create the life that you desire. So you will unconsciously or consciously settle for a relationship because it feels like it gives you the validation you're seeking, one that likely fulfills the unmet needs of your inner child or teenager.

During your karmic relationship, being able to discover who you are, to feel free to live life, and to make decisions for yourself will be the lessons that come up the most frequently. Either you will choose someone who can give you the feelings for yourself that you haven't yet developed, or else you will be in a relationship where you feel so needed at the beginning that you talk yourself out of wanting more. Wanting more doesn't mean that you need something better than what you have — it simply means you desire a relationship that is more in alignment with your own truth.

In the karmic relationship you will feel restricted and even lost at times. This could lead to substance use, multiple relationships, and emotional manipulation through guilt to keep you from traversing the path of your truth. The more that you can embrace your truth and focus on your emotional, mental, spiritual, and physical health, the more you will naturally grow out of this relationship.

Your truth, which you must learn for yourself, is all you need to know: that you were always worthy of the life and love that you dream of.

The South Node in Capricorn

Your Karmic Lesson Affirmation: *I am able to change my mind and grow so that I can create space for a healthy and fulfilling relationship.*

You can do everything right in your karmic connection, but when you have the South Node in Capricorn, in the end, it doesn't mean that this partnership will ever actually *feel* right for you. In your karmic relationship, you will be faced with examining your beliefs, conditioning, and choices to assess whether they are helping you create the life that you desire or whether, instead, they are preventing you from living it. The South Node in Capricorn is all about the rules — the societal and familial conditioning and expectations for how you should live your life. These rules especially come into play when children are involved in your relationship.

Breakup or divorce likely seems impossible in the beginning of this phase and even feels like something you would be punished for; it will look like the only option for you is to continue on, even after you acknowledge your unhappiness. The individual you attract in the karmic relationship will challenge you to see that there is more to life than you thought. This individual could even be the very definition of a free spirit, providing you with a mirror of all that is possible as you struggle to do what you think is right while also pursuing your happiness. Your inner conflict and what you will be tasked with overcoming would be showing up as inconsistency in your relationship, your own avoidance or reluctance, or you burying yourself in your work. You will continually try to return to your rule book of life, even if nothing is working out as planned.

Your lesson comes in choosing between nurturing your own growth and happiness, on the one hand, and upholding your obligations and responsibilities, on the other. Ultimately, you are meant to learn that the only valid rules are those based on your truth. Sometimes that means you have to break a few, including those made by people whom you love.

As you expand your mind to include different possibilities and outcomes, you also are able to define what your own truth is and become willing to embrace it. That, ultimately, is what will allow you to transition out of this relationship and into a life of greater balance.

The South Node in Aquarius

Your Karmic Lesson Affirmation: *I am powerful in my authenticity and am able to create the life of my dreams.*

Aquarius is the sign of the rebel, the revolutionary, the one who lives by the beat of their own drum. Yet if your South Node is in Aquarius, to fully realize this power, you first need to feel the pangs of restriction. To learn your karmic lesson, you will enter into a relationship with someone who asks you to conform in order to earn their love and attention. This usually occurs because you've lost your internal compass. You struggle to find stability and the acceptance of others, and so you create a relationship where you are offered all of that — but at the expense of your self.

In your karmic relationship, you will constantly feel that you can't measure up, that no matter what you do, it's never enough for your partner — nor are they enough for you. With your deep desire for acceptance, you may choose a partner who has narcissistic tendencies, as they will condition you to seek their approval at any cost.

You will go through a period of feeling trapped within your relationship and doubtful about your ability to transition out of it. However, the light at the end of the tunnel will become apparent as you start to recognize that what you really need is your own approval to follow your unique path.

Instead of feeling like you have to give up the best parts of yourself, reflect on your strengths and other qualities. Understand why you thought you had to do things a certain way in order to receive validation from others and how deeply people-pleasing was ingrained in you as a means to get approval.

The more that you can create acceptance for yourself, build up your inner sense of worth, validate your truth, and allow yourself to set boundaries with those who are comfortable with you only if you stay the same, the more deeply you will be able to heal.

The South Node in Pisces

Your Karmic Lesson Affirmation: *I am able to radiate both love and healthy boundaries while being open to receiving what I deserve.*

As one of the softer signs of the zodiac, people with the South Node in Pisces often choose self-preservation over hard decisions, even if in the long run it becomes a detriment. If this is you, your lesson will be to learn that the reality of your karmic relationship is far different from the dream that you had.

The South Node is vastly unlike the emotional water sign of Pisces, so this relationship becomes difficult territory to navigate. While the South Node seeks to create boundaries, Pisces only wants love. And while the South Node wants to learn, Pisces only wants to dream. Yet by moving through the lesson of this relationship, you will be able to build the kind of love that you truly desire.

During this phase of your life, you will likely attract someone who takes advantage of you. Whether it be in the realm of emotional energy, housing, or finances, your karmic relationship will drain you until it feels like you can't continue. You tend to attract partners who need you, which appeals to your empathetic nature — but it's also the only way you can learn the boundaries that healthy love requires. During this relationship, you may create chaos for yourself by trying to give your partner everything they ask for or need; likely you won't even wait for them to voice their wants but will simply offer to fulfill them as readily as you do your heart.

Your karmic relationship may bring in unhealthy qualities, such as abuse, codependency, or control, because to learn the lessons of the South Node in Pisces you need to be challenged to step into your own power, instead of remaining in the dream world you prefer. There will be many chances to step into your healing through betrayals and hurts in this connection as you struggle to understand why no matter what you give, it never seems to make a difference.

Ultimately, your lesson comes down to your beliefs about having to earn love, which likely are rooted in rejection and abandonment that you experienced earlier in life. That, coupled with your inability to create healthy boundaries and a lack of your own self-worth, creates the perfect karmic storm.

Try to get space from this relationship as you heal and rebuild your life. The more you can recognize that you deserve all the love and kindness you extend to others, the more deeply you can fulfill your own needs. You may want to be loved, but if what you're getting does not match the way that you genuinely need to be loved, then that feeling of lack will always exist.

Come back to your own self, your true worth. As you begin to learn that boundaries actually create a space for love to grow, you will feel strong enough to transition out of this relationship and into the place to receive what you truly desire.

The Significance of the
Developed and Undeveloped Chart

Maturity isn't reached simply because you go through puberty or reach the age of adulthood. Instead, it's found through the ability to confront your childhood lessons, heal, and stop allowing wounds and conditioning to influence your personal truth.

To physically mature is one thing, but to reach the point of maturity within the soul is another.

In birth charts, especially when we're comparing the charts of romantic partners, a pivotal moment occurs when one or both people have reached the point of a *developed chart*.

For every planetary position in your natal chart — that is, the zodiac sign each planet is in at the time of your birth — you'll find both positives (the best possible influences) and negatives (the largest challenges). Instead of looking at them both as influences you will always have to contend with, you can actually embrace more of the positives once you have learned your karmic lesson. This is what transforms your natal chart into a developed chart.

For instance, if you have your Neptune in Pisces, you will have at your grasp a huge capacity for spiritual well-being and unconditional love; however, you also can run the risk of disillusionment, substance abuse, or living in a fantasy world. Whether you have an undeveloped or a developed chart will make all the difference in which energies you are able to embrace.

This has nothing to do with age or with how much knowledge

you have about astrology; it's all about whether or not you've learned your Saturn and South Node lessons. When you have, this is the point when you reach soul maturity and also when you can harness the positives of your birth chart without being held back by its obstacles.

When you have learned your karmic lesson, you change your vibration. You become more aware, taking greater responsibility for what has shaped your existence in this life. You also are now fully embodying truth: the truth of what you came into this life with, the truth of what you experienced in childhood, and the truth of what you have unconsciously been searching for or playing out within your romantic relationships. This shift is what makes the biggest difference in your life.

Before I focused my counseling practice on relationships and love, I first started working with clients on how to be happier — how to fill their life with more of what they wanted and less of what they felt like they "had" to do.

What I found was that I could spend hours asking about their career, themselves, or anything else in their life, but it was always their romantic relationship that provided the biggest moments of clarity.

A romantic relationship isn't just about companionship or romance; it represents where you are at with yourself, because it's the one area in which you can't pretend. Your romantic relationship truly is the barometer for your life. Without it, you wouldn't even be aware of your karmic lesson or of the significance of the developed and undeveloped chart. That's because only in the soft vulnerability of love do your defenses come down, and you are triggered in such a way that you forget about pretending to be okay or trying to have it all figured out.

Your relationship with another is simply a mirror for the one you have with yourself and with the universe. Regardless of your spiritual beliefs (if any), everything in this world is connected through a force of energy, which is what the power of attraction is based on. Your power to achieve more, to attract better, ultimately always is determined by your soul's maturity. And that maturity is only to be found by learning the lessons of Saturn and the South Node you are meant to learn in this life.

The Hope of the Undeveloped

When you are truly tuned into the universe and to the greater meaning that exists in life, you'll see the world in less black and white terms. Nothing is really bad, and that also means nothing is fully good; every experience holds something to learn, something to take away as the gold to make your soul shine even brighter.

The *undeveloped chart* isn't bad: it's what we all enter into life with as the map of possibilities for the experiences we will attract. It shows you where you will struggle, but also where your success will be found. It helps you to understand the parts of yourself you can work on to heal and grow; it also points the way to the rewards of those efforts.

When you are born, your natal chart describes the exact point where every planet was at precisely the moment you entered this life. Yet nothing is a given, because you have free will; you will forge your individual path. And to actually become the person you were meant to be in this life, healing and growth can't be thrust upon you, but instead must be consciously chosen.

The undeveloped chart helps you to become aware of what to work on within yourself in order to embrace the power of control you possess over yourself and your life. For instance, if you have Mercury in Aries, then in the undeveloped chart, you might be prone to anger and shutting down, which only complicates your life. But as you learn, as you grow, embracing more and more of your lessons in your karmic relationship, you'll be able to control your reactions and bring forth the natural influence and leadership you carry. Your karmic lesson is to understand that you have a choice at all, because this relationship creates a situation where you are under the illusion you have none.

One of the main reasons the karmic relationship lasts so long is that as long as you are still learning, you also often give away your power to your partner. You imagine it's their choice to walk away or to commit, to change, to go all in, because you're not ready to stand in your own power. You make it all about them, when in reality it's actually all about you.

As long as you are in the undeveloped phase of your life, pushing off those lessons, hoping the other person will do the work or make the decisions, you're not doing your own divine work. Your karmic relationship forces you to embrace your inner power, to stop abandoning yourself, and to decide what you are willing to accept and what you aren't. Now you can create boundaries, not to keep people out but to be treated in the sacred manner you deserve.

It's Not You — It's Me

About a year ago I began working with a gentleman named Hayden, who felt like he'd done everything possible to better himself and the relationship he was in. He was married to Lydia, with children, and while he was taking responsibility for himself, he just couldn't understand why nothing seemed to make a difference in his relationship.

He admitted he was prone to anger in the relationship, although throughout his life, his manner had normally been calm and mild. This was the only area in his life where he'd felt so frustrated and upset that he became someone he normally wasn't, inclined to shouting and grumpiness. As he became aware of his behavior, he sought counseling from a therapist and began the deep journey of self-work, but even that didn't seem to change how he felt at home or the disconnect in his marriage.

One of the most interesting aspects that arose was his reluctance to see the significance of this relationship being the only situation that had ever triggered loudness and anger from him. Lydia had taught him to hold guilt and shame around that behavior, which had never been a part of his personality before.

As we continued to dive into the story of his life, an important truth emerged regarding how he had spoken and lived his truth prior and how those themes were currently being challenged in his relationship. Hayden began to understand he was actually becoming so angry and loud, not because of his current situation, but because he was trying to hear his own truth.

The longer this relationship continued, the more it felt like it wasn't in alignment with his growth, yet he was loath to admit that because of his fears about raising children in two separate households. He wanted to do everything possible to avoid having his children deal with a separation. However, it seemed things were only continuing to deteriorate. And so the anger and frustration built. Not just toward his partner, but most importantly toward himself, because he was betraying himself by remaining in this relationship.

After we spoke a few times, I suggested taking a look at his and Lydia's astrology charts, just to see if they would provide any clarity — and of course, as always, the stars obliged.

Right away I noticed that Hayden had his Mercury in Aries, and now the behavior he had been describing suddenly started to make sense. The reason he was stuck in anger was not just because he needed to more deeply honor his truth. This relationship was his karmic connection, which was meant to help his soul mature into the developed chart.

HAYDEN	
Sun	Aries
Moon	Capricorn
Mercury	Aries
Venus	Taurus
Mars	Aries
Jupiter	Sagittarius
Saturn	Scorpio
Uranus	Sagittarius
Neptune	Sagittarius
Pluto	Libra
North Node	Gemini
South Node	Sagittarius
Rising	Cancer

LYDIA	
Sun	Leo
Moon	Aquarius
Mercury	Leo
Venus	Leo
Mars	Leo
Jupiter	Aries
Saturn	Sagittarius
Uranus	Sagittarius
Neptune	Capricorn
Pluto	Libra
North Node	Aries
South Node	Libra
Rising	Sagittarius

Hayden and Lydia also represent an interesting dynamic because, while this was a karmic relationship for Hayden, for Lydia it originally appeared to be a relationship that would be all that she wanted, with her North Node in Aries reflecting Hayden's sun in Aries. But this is a lesson that just because something may appear perfect to your ego doesn't necessarily mean that is what it will ultimately become. This dynamic represents one of the more challenging aspects in romantic relationships, as sometimes it is easier if both people are each other's karmic relationship. However, in this case, Hayden and Lydia each viewed their relationship in vastly different ways, and that was backed up by what the astrology charts illustrated.

In breaking down their charts a bit more, I was first drawn to Hayden's South Node in Sagittarius and saw that was the zodiac sign that Lydia's Saturn was in, automatically signifying this was a karmic connection for him. However, his sun sign, Aries, was both her North Node and her Jupiter sign, which represents fate, the future, and abundance.

For Lydia, this was a healing relationship of the ego that allowed her to learn more about herself. Not only was a great deal of similar fire energy present between them, but she was also drawn to the characteristics that she unconsciously believed represented fate, abundance, and the life that she dreamed of. However, because Lydia's Saturn was Hayden's South Node sign, they were supposed to learn different lessons. With Saturn representing the personal karma, Lydia's lesson centered around herself and uncovering her autonomy, while Hayden's South Node in Sagittarius guided him to move through generational and inner child healing as he became able to make decisions that were more authentic for him.

The lesson of the South Node in Sagittarius for Hayden was about him allowing himself to be loved for exactly who he was, as well as having the freedom to continue to explore his own personal journey. Lydia, with her North Node and Jupiter in Aries, actually needed to learn how to embody greater autonomy and authenticity within herself first and to speak her truth about the misalignment of this relationship.

Hayden also provides the perfect example of what happens in an undeveloped chart. With his Mercury (communication) in the fire sign of Aries, the very behaviors he spoke of are precisely what would be triggered, especially as he began to learn more of his soul lessons in this lifetime and from this particular relationship. In this sense, although he wanted to remain married for a common reason — his children — he was physically somewhere that his soul had already grown out of.

Sometimes the difference between one partner emerging as a developed chart (Hayden) while the other is still in the midst of their undeveloped chart (Lydia) is unbridgeable. While there are always suggestions in couples counseling to help improve romantic relationships, something I often speak about is that there is a difference between healing a simple disconnect from the circumstances of life and attempting to create a connection that was never there in the first place.

More often than not, if people are honest with themselves, they approach couples counseling looking to create a feeling, an energy, or a dynamic that perhaps never existed but that, through their own growth, they've come to recognize they need. When this happens, it's because one person in the relationship has reached the point of becoming a developed chart, just as Hayden had, and is hoping to be able to change not only the relationship but also the other person.

Ultimately, for Hayden, this journey was about arriving at his own acceptance of himself and what he really needed from love. It required him to heal his childhood wounds and prioritize himself while he learned to trust that the most important thing for his children was to have parents who were free to heal, grow, and become their best selves, even if that had to be done separately.

As he moved through the process, he also realized that there was a middle ground between silencing his truth and having to shout to be heard. Many times, when we are in relationships in which the purpose is to trigger major soul growth, we will exhibit uncharacteristic behaviors solely in that dynamic, such as anger or yelling in this case. As Hayden practiced speaking up more, allowing himself to align his external life with his internal growth, he found he didn't feel as angry and discovered a new peace within himself.

The Morning After

As you progress through your karmic relationship, there is a moment when it feels like the light returns in a sudden whoosh of clarity as you realize how long you've put up with behavior or circumstances that don't feel good or resonate with your soul. But it's not enough to just have one shining moment of clarity. To step into a healthy lasting relationship, firmly closing the door on everything that is now behind you, is the larger task.

Transforming your undeveloped chart into a developed one means you absorb the brilliant moment of clarity, you move through the lesson, and you take on whatever it means to incorporate that glimmer of truth, no matter how small, into your life. Just as it's not enough to simply say you want a divorce — you actually have to go through the process of filing for one — the same is true for this phase of your life.

At this point it will feel uncomfortable, as you're likely taking your first tentative steps toward self-worth and truth. You are testing what you've learned by having faith in yourself, which is the first step to owning your personal power and taking back everything you've given away to others.

As you move forward, it becomes easier, because by learning your karmic lesson, you also are opening up a new path of growth. You are having to stretch yourself in new ways without proof it will pay off; you only know that remaining where you are is no longer possible. Now you are following a feeling and trusting it, even if you don't know where this is all going to lead.

You are more open to the truth, to being okay with upsetting others or not living up to their expectations of you. Because while this is the path of light, it doesn't mean you won't end up playing the villain in someone else's story. Integrating your karmic lesson means you're okay with that. It means you no longer try to control the narrative of how you're seen, because you are learning that to accept and love yourself is all that matters.

And as you do, this new way of life becomes one you don't have to try so hard at. Boundaries come like second nature, and self-validation fuels you to reach for the stars. Your soul has begun its important healing and has matured to a place where you no longer need to repeat the lessons of your past — because you've outgrown the person you once were.

The Peace of the Developed Chart

As a new era of being settles within your soul, you find a deep sense of self-acceptance for all you've been through. You no longer hold onto regrets like pieces of broken glass that continue to cause pain, because you've freed yourself from thinking anything could or should have been different.

No longer are you asking yourself, *Why did this happen to me?* Instead, you're thinking, *Look at what I've become because of all I've been through. Look at these fires that I stepped into so I could transform into a higher version of myself* — which for any of us means that we're no longer living through our wounds, but instead we're embracing life as a mature soul, with an open heart and truth-seeking eyes.

Understanding the relationship you're in is karmic is one step. Seeing that you have an undeveloped chart because you're still in the process of learning is another. But on this journey of self-growth, there is the idea of a great awakening. Once you have fully awakened, you can't return to the slumber of who you were, no matter how much you wish you could.

There is only forward, even if the path is shrouded in the fog of the unknown.

So you continue on, you move through your karmic relationship, and you begin to honor your inner power by recognizing your self-worth, embracing your truth, and taking on the challenging moments in life. And as you do, things continue to change around and within you. And suddenly you don't see anything as insurmountable any longer. What previously felt like obstacles instead are just moments of growth to experience.

And Just Like That...It's Over

In the developed chart, you have learned your karmic lesson from the South Node and Saturn, thereby healing your childhood wounds, putting boundaries in place, and severing that thread of connection to your karmic partner, which was only there to hold you in place long enough to learn what you were meant to.

One of the most interesting aspects of the karmic connection and the developed chart is the suddenness with which that soul bind isn't just cut but moved past with ease once the lesson has truly been learned. This feeling of not being able to escape the connection is one of the hallmark traits of the karmic relationship. We think it means we are supposed to be together, but in reality, it's so strong because in that moment it is where we are meant to be.

In my work with individuals who are in their karmic relationship stage, I've seen how challenging it can be. Until we are ready for the truth, we will be unable to see it or even hear it from another. But I honor that process. I have to, just as you have to for yourself. In this connection, it's not about doing what you logically think is right; instead, it's about moving through it until your wounds or inner child are no longer attracted to that relationship.

We can become angry and shout at our karmic partner that we

never want to see them again, but as long as the lesson this relationship offers is still unlearned, we will always find ourselves back in the same place, because to learn this lesson we have to let our inner child move through it fully. This relationship, more than any other, is the one that will help you heal all you've been through — and maybe even heal the wounds of past generations as well.

This process became especially evident in my work with one of my clients, Isabella.

When Isabella first came to me, it was under the guise of helping her and her twin flame come together in a healthy and stable relationship. However, as we talked through her history and looked at the truth of her romantic connection, it seemed that this relationship was much more reflective of her childhood trauma and wounds than of the divine, healthy soul love that is associated with a twin flame relationship.

But Isabella wasn't ready to hear that, despite the fact that we reviewed the astrology charts for both her and her romantic interest, Alejandro, many times — until finally, years after we began, she suddenly pointed out the very patterns I had always described to her.

What made this process difficult for Isabella was that both her North Node and her Saturn were in Aries. That meant there were two perspectives from which she could view this relationship with Alejandro: she could see it as her ultimate love, or she could understand it as a final lesson that would get her to the place to attract what she had always desired.

When she first came to me, she was leading with her wounds, and so her inner child saw no other option than to believe this was the man meant for her. As she moved through her healing, stepped into her worthiness, and started to focus more on the patterns in her connection with Alejandro as well as what actually went into a healthy, stable relationship, she began to see things differently. She was starting to move from the undeveloped into the developed chart.

ALEJANDRO	
Sun	Aries
Moon	Capricorn
Mercury	Aries
Venus	Gemini
Mars	Gemini
Jupiter	Capricorn
Saturn	Gemini
Uranus	Libra
Neptune	Sagittarius
Pluto	Libra
North Node	Aquarius
South Node	Leo
Rising	Aries

ISABELLA	
Sun	Scorpio
Moon	Aquarius
Mercury	Scorpio
Venus	Virgo
Mars	Capricorn
Jupiter	Virgo
Saturn	Aries
Uranus	Virgo
Neptune	Scorpio
Pluto	Virgo
North Node	Aries
South Node	Libra
Rising	Gemini

In one pivotal moment of awakening, she suddenly saw with striking clarity how similar this was to past relationships, as well as how it played into her childhood dynamic and wounds. She literally felt repulsed by the relationship and no longer wanted to spend time with Alejandro. In that moment, she was able to embody her lesson so deeply, she broke the soul bind that had kept her in that relationship and ushered in an entirely new phase of life.

And although she still had to complete the process of removing different layers of conditioning that her inner child carried, she was over him, finished with the cycle, and just like that...she was free.

One of the strongest aspects in Isabella and Alejandro's charts was that her Saturn sign was reflected in his sun and Mercury sign. That meant it wasn't just how he moved through life and who she perceived him to be that were going to be pivotal in her learning the lesson associated with this relationship, but also conversations and his personal thought process would be important to that learning.

While her North Node and Saturn were both in Aries, it never meant there would be only one relationship that did the work of both. Many times in cases such as this, once the Saturn soulmate lesson has been learned, the person might attract a partner whose Venus or Jupiter are in Aries, representing the fate of her North Node through how she will be loved or the abundant future they will create together. This would allow her to not only move through her Saturn lesson but also fully embody her fate as she stepped into a place of greater sovereignty and attracted the very thing she'd always desired.

One of the important things to know in working with the karmic relationship is that only in the developed chart phase does this relationship fully dissolve out of your life. So many times we hear people talk of clearing karma or breaking a soul tie; you can find a great deal of spells, remedies, and expensive ceremonies that promise to do just that. However, this relationship comes into your life for a purpose: not just to heal you but to help you mature into your higher self. That means nothing in the human realm will be able to break the tie other than learning what you're meant to learn.

In all honesty, I tried breaking my own karmic connection at all costs. I traveled the world and sat with every medicine man, shaman, and spiritual worker I could find to help me leave behind what I knew was not healthy or in alignment with the person I was becoming. In one particular instance, I spent time around a bonfire in the mountains of central Guatemala with a Mayan shaman, who also appeared to be the mystical grandmother we all wish we had.

As the late afternoon sun glinted off her silver hair and the scent of cedar filled the air, I watched her come slowly down the path, a knobby wooden cane in one hand and a sack with unknown items over her other shoulder. She unpacked her herbs and candles, and we sat around the fire on logs worn smooth, the tall, ancient trees providing protection from all that existed outside of our circle. Immediately she said she knew why I was there. She told me the energy I had around me would take everything from me if I let it; she knew there was darkness in it. She also let me know that I had to love myself more than I thought I loved him.

I lost track of time as we sat there talking, burning candles and oil, the sun continuing its descent in the sky, until finally she asked me to get up for the next part of the ceremony. After anointing a bouquet of herbs meant to banish this man out of my life, she used smoke to cleanse my energy points and repeatedly hit the herbs against me, paying special attention to my sacral chakra area to cleanse his sexual energy from my body.

As I left reeking of smoke, spattered in herbs and candle wax, the *agua de florida* still dripping through my hair, I thought maybe it had worked. But when my karmic connection texted me that evening, I knew it hadn't. I finally understood that no matter how much I felt I was on the path to my destruction, I had to keep going — the only way out really was through.

And, like Isabella and Hayden, I realized it in my own time. No one had been able to tell me differently, because it was something I needed to feel, to experience, for myself. I could get to the point where I could stop repeating something I already knew was bad for me only when I learned my karmic lesson: that I didn't need anyone to prove I was worthy of being loved. I had finally done that for myself.

Moving into the developed chart means now you have the ability to cocreate what you desire with the universe, as you no longer deny your truth or need that old storyline to prove you are worthy, special, chosen by another. You shift your understanding of validation from something you need to get from others to something you offer yourself. By making that shift, you start to see how to work with the universe and your own divine gifts.

When you adopt the developed chart in your life, you now have the best of everything at your fingertips. Say, for example, you've become aware you have a short temper; however, you've also learned you become triggered when you are withholding your truth or someone is limiting you from speaking or living it. And so when you feel your temper triggered, you pause, you breathe into it, and maybe you even count to ten. You remind yourself that you aren't who you used to be and this isn't like before. You are safe. You are continuously healing. And because of that, you can choose to act or react differently than before.

This is what opens the doorway to your next chapter, the one where you get to attract what is truly in alignment with your soul and with the fate that was always written in the stars.

Finding Balance

Our karmic relationship is really the ultimate teacher in so many ways. Not only does it help heal our wounds, but it also helps us see clearly who we authentically are and what we need from a relationship. This phase is when it seems we grow up and are ready to leave behind the self-sacrifice and excuses of our inner child. But that's not the sole gift of this connection. In this phase, we also come to recognize the idea of balance and what it means for us. Not only the balance we feel internally, but also that which we seek to create in our life.

Balance isn't equal; it doesn't mean we give precisely the same investment of time to each area of our lives or that we give of ourselves to every person in our lives in the same way. It means that, because we have moved through the lessons we needed to learn, we can feel free to create the definition of balance that works best for us.

In astrology, though, balance has a particular meaning. Here balance is determined by how each of the four elements is present in your birth chart — basically, the number of air, earth, fire, and water placements that you have. It's also reflected in the charts of those you are attracted to, and it will show up in specific ways if you're still looking for something you haven't yet given yourself. Early in your journey, many times the elements in your partner's chart will be representative of one of your parents or caregivers in childhood. After moving through the phase of the developed chart, however, you will tend to seek out what will help bring greater balance into your life.

External balance can be achieved only once you have created internal balance for yourself. To create internal balance, the first step is knowledge — knowing what it means, for instance, if you lack any earth or water placements. By understanding this aspect of your chart, you will be able to take responsibility for understanding yourself more deeply and also for correcting some of the challenges your chart may bring.

While you are precisely as you are meant to be in this lifetime, understanding yourself more deeply will only create greater success for you and any relationships you have. Even reaching the developed chart phase doesn't mean there isn't anything else to learn or that you have achieved a state of perfection. Instead, it opens up your awareness, so you aren't just honoring your karmic lesson but also recognizing that this journey of life contains constant lessons. It doesn't mean life will always be challenging or bring you to your knees in tears, but that you will be given opportunities to take who you authentically are and explore ways to become better, which really translates to becoming healthier.

When you are healthy, not just in your physical body but in your heart, mind, and soul, then you enter the space to do things differently than before. This means that you will start to recognize red flags before they even make their appearance and that you will know what it is you need and will be able to advocate for that in relationships.

As with any process, though, the first step is always understanding, because the more you can understand your inner self, the more profound the love will be that you can create with another.

No One Completes You — but You

Each person's astrology is unique, simply because everyone's birth chart is different, just as their personal wounds are. Yet there are common themes that carry through in similar ways for everyone. This is especially true in the configuration of your elements. No matter what's happening elsewhere in your chart, having at least one placement each in fire, water, earth, and air will help you not only to feel more balanced but also to find greater success in your life.

But you will not always have each element present in your birth chart. In some charts, a piece is missing. This creates an absence of the particular energy of the missing element. And when a piece is missing, often your default setting will be to seek out someone who can fill that empty space.

To discover where this present is for you, look at your birth chart and see where it lists the elements and the number next to each one. (If you birth chart doesn't include that information, you can make a list for yourself by referring to "Identifying the Elements of Each Zodiac Sign" in the glossary in the back of this book.) This number represents the planetary bodies in your chart that are within that element. To find your *leading element* — the element that is strongest in your chart — look for the highest number. In the process, also take note of whether there is an absence of any element. Both the leading element and any absence of an element affect your personality and what you attract.

What is so fascinating is that your sun sign doesn't determine your leading element. For instance, I am a Pisces sun sign (and even Cancer rising — both water placements), yet my leading element is air, with the majority of my placements in that area. This vastly changes the meaning of my chart and what I attract. It also challenges any traditional ideas about the perfect astrological match for me as a Pisces, because a Pisces with a leading air element will be different from those who have a leading earth or water element. The sun sign determines only one area of your personality, often how you are seen by others, while your leading element makes up more of your authentic nature. Your leading element is actually what will determine your greatest strengths and compatibility when attracting a romantic partner.

When you understand how to work with your own personal leading element, you also become aware of why perhaps you've felt different from other people with your same sun sign. Your leading element helps you to make sense of events and situations in your life. But most importantly, by understanding this piece of yourself, which is what the karmic relationship is all about, it enables you to see the kind of love you truly need.

While an aspect of complementary energy goes into all healthy partnerships, the key is first to be able to work with your own limitations, rather than just attracting someone to fill a conscious or unconscious lack. For instance, if you have no planetary placements in air, you may attract a karmic partner who has a leading air element. However, if you haven't yet found what motivates you or how to muster up the follow-through to make a dream a reality — two themes of the air element — then you will only end up draining your partner. You may even feel like you are dependent upon your partner, simply because you haven't learned to work your own lacks rather than seeking what you're lacking in another.

As long as we are perceiving a lack in ourselves, either consciously or unconsciously, we will only ever attract relationships that mirror the lessons we still have to learn for ourselves.

The Meaning of the Elements

Each element represents an important part of your life and affects how you make decisions. For example, if you are preparing to make a shift to a new job, relationship, or country, each element provides a resource for you, and together they go into the process as a whole.

If it's a new job you are seeking, it's the air element that will come up with the idea for it. The earth element will help you create the plan and foundation for it. Fire will inspire you to take action. And the water element will continually guide you to check in to see how you are feeling about things, so you do not deviate from your truth.

Depending on your leading element, you may be better at creating an idea, making a plan, taking action, or looking at the emotional implications of whatever change you are creating. Conversely, if there is an absence in your chart, it can feel as if an important step is missing in the process. You may be able to create what you desire in your life, but until you are aware of what step is missing, situations will feel more challenging than you might want.

All this, of course, is especially true in a romantic relationship. Each of the elements plays a significant role in the love you choose. For instance, someone with a leading air element would be thinking about where the relationship might be going, while someone with leading earth would be responsible for creating a plan to keep growing together. A person with leading fire would keep inspiring action and have the ability to introduce new elements to the relationship. And an individual with leading water would be emotionally sensitive and ensure that their choices were in alignment with their feelings.

You are made of the stars and all the planets, but you are also made from the earth, fire, air, and water. To find your balance, you must understand what natural characteristics you are working with and be proactive in appropriate ways. If you happen to have an absence of water, for instance, you may need to be more aware of your own feelings or your partner's, while an absence of earth would remind you of the importance of grounding and slowing down your thought process.

The most important thing about astrology, and specifically your elements, is that whatever negative story you've been telling yourself about life and especially about love, that story doesn't have to be true. It doesn't have to be the reality you live by, because by learning and being committed to becoming a better and healthier version of yourself, you can change your story. With that comes the ability not just to live the life you've always desired but also to attract that delicious, soulful, healthy love you want into your life.

The Air Element

Air Affirmation: *I am creative, open-minded, and capable of creating whatever I dream.*

Leading Air

Air is the element that rules the mind, which means that in many ways, your thought process is one of your greatest strengths. To have a leading air element makes your mind very active, both in how you think about things and in your ability to express yourself. You tend to be very intellectual, even if you haven't gone through traditional schooling, and you are always looking for a better way to do things. An air element will naturally have an amazing selection of ideas, some very grandiose and others that seem inherently unique to you.

In romance, a leading air element rarely dates just for fun; instead, you must have a purpose. Regardless of what your ultimate desires are for a relationship, you tend to date for a specific goal or dream. It might be marriage, or it may be a profound romantic connection, but you have a very particular idea of what you are looking for and have no desire to entertain anything less. In this case, having a partner who understands your desire for planning and fulfilling your dreams is incredibly important, and you can often find great success in a relationship with a partner who has a leading earth or fire element — as long as there is actually planning in place and not just the dream of it.

The most important soul lesson for a leading air placement is to learn to trust in your ideas and desires for whatever you imagine. This element can conceive of things that have never before been done and is able to create almost anything they dream, but believing in themselves is a necessary prerequisite for that. When you finally believe in yourself, you become an unstoppable force in any area that you desire and can also create the relationship you've always sought.

Absence of Air

When your chart has an absence of the element of air, life can feel frustrating until you are able to recognize what your true strength is. To lack air in your chart doesn't mean you won't have ideas, but you will have a challenging time trusting those thoughts you do have and being able to choose just one. In this case, you likely have a surplus of energy in another element, so you will need to coach yourself to take time to figure things out through a slower and more detail-oriented process.

Without any planets in air, you may desire to move, change relationships, or make some other change, but you still find yourself in the same place you were a decade ago. To help yourself work with the absence of an energy, first determine your strength. Is it being able to make plans, take action, or feel emotionally connected to life around you? Once you know what your strength is, you can work with your lack of air energy by journaling about what you desire for your life and then asking yourself if what you've come up with feels like part of your truth.

As I mentioned, the soul lesson for a leading air is to believe in themselves; it's actually a similar lesson for those with an absence of air. Even with that absence, you have dreams and ideas for what you want your life and especially your relationship to become, but you need to slow down your thought process, choose which dream or idea you will focus on, limit distractions, and practice self-validation.

In your relationship, you have to be mindful that you may be leaning on your partner to take the lead too often; you need to ensure that you are doing your part to bring balance to your connection. When the dynamic is unbalanced, your partner can become the one who always has to plan dates or trips, the one who continually progresses your relationship to the next level. To create a healthier situation, you will want to plan something once a month for yourself and your partner, perhaps take charge of accommodations or restaurants when you are going on a trip together. While it feels good to have a partner who can plan and provide direction, recognize that you need to consciously work through your own limitations to do that a bit yourself so the relationship will feel more balanced for each of you.

The Fire Element

Fire Affirmation: *I am confident, strong, and trust myself to choose what is best for me and others.*

Leading Fire

As a leading fire element, you breathe passion into each area of your life. You are determined, focused, and tend to embrace freedom more ardently than others. This allows you to be a leader in your life, as you have no problem leaping before you look or trusting that things will somehow always work out in your favor. Your greatest strength is that you do not let a single moment or opportunity pass you by. Fire rules the action you take, so physicality is extremely important to you. While air may rule the mind, your element rules the way in which you move in the world.

In relationships, you tend to prefer to take the lead, as you have a specific desire for your connection and how to manifest what you want. You enjoy planning and creating special moments for yourself and your partner; however, you tend to be more spontaneous than looking at things in the long term. Romantically, for you, it's important to choose a relationship to help bring out your greatest strengths rather than one that will only try to put out your fire. Because of your ability to lead, to take action, and to embrace your passion, having a partner who responds to all of those qualities instead of one who wants to do the same will allow there to be a greater balance in your connection. It's common for leading fire elements to be attracted to those who are the same, but it usually can lead to significant arguments, as both people want to lead or fulfill their passions for life. Having a partner who is softer and who desires someone else to take action or to lead will be important, so an air or water element could work well for you, especially if you are dedicated to developing your own emotional intelligence.

As a fire element, your soul lesson rests in being confident about the decisions and choices you make. In life, events rarely go according to plan. While everyone has to go through this process, for a leading fire element it can result in the overquestioning of everything to the point that you ignore your own nature. Understanding that something not working out the way you'd hoped is part of finding what will. You need to learn not to take moments of loss or heartbreak personally, so you can still embrace your innate sense of confidence. While you often learn the value of planning things out a bit and moderating any impulsiveness, your passion and desire are among your greatest strengths. It's important to embrace that and never forget you truly do hold the power to create the life you desire.

Absence of Fire

To have an absence of fire energy means that it can be very challenging to feel sure enough about yourself to take any action. You might have the most amazing ideas and even be able to plan things out with remarkable precision, but still something holds you back from taking action to become all that you dream of. Without knowing that you have an absence of fire energy, you likely will be hard on yourself, as you mistakenly think this is a personal defect instead of something that can be navigated around.

Without any fire energy in your chart, you struggle to believe in yourself, to trust the process of change, and to find confidence in your abilities. But these are issues that you can work on. If you know that you have an absence of the fire element, personal work around self-worth and confidence, as well as pushing yourself beyond your comfort zone, will be incredibly important. The more that you know you are worthy of your dreams, the more confident you will become in taking chances. It can also be effective for you to break actions down into smaller steps. When you can receive validation from taking smaller steps and reaping success, then you can build up your confidence for the bigger ones.

In relationships, you need to ensure that you're not self-sabotaging, which can lead to sabotaging your connection. Without fire energy, you may not feel like you deserve your partner, or you can't envision how your lives would ever align. But recognize that the love and connection you feel aren't only real, but they're a reflection of who you are. Practice saying affirmations about your worthiness in love, and just as you would for a big job change, focus on the smaller steps you can take to build the relationship you desire. Push yourself away from your comfort zone a bit and make suggestions for plans, advocate for what you need, or share how you struggle to follow through. One of the most important things to be mindful of is that you can be fully in love with your partner and see a life with them, but they might not necessarily feel that from you. Check in, providing positive affirmations and validation to your partner about your commitment. The more confident you are, the more you attract what you've always wanted from life.

The Earth Element

Earth Affirmation: *I am grounded and feel safe to take risks. I explore my life path with success and security.*

Leading Earth

As a leading earth element, you have the divine gift of being able to plan out and create solid foundations in your life. This means that unless you deliberately choose to go in a different direction or dismantle something, whatever you create always has the potential to last forever and produce a great deal of abundance. With strong earth placements, you excel in building a bridge between an initial idea and the actions needed to carry it out. For you, feeling secure, safe, and stable in whatever you are creating is essential, which means sometimes you struggle with leaving your comfort zone. It's not that you don't want to, but safety is your number one priority, and often safety can translate to sameness.

In romantic relationships, you tend to do very well with partners who are looking for a highly committed relationship. As a leading earth element, you will focus on creating a solid foundation for your life together. Whether it's progressing through dating in a traditional way or securing a down payment on a home before going to showings, everything you do is truly built from the ground up. This works extremely well in a relationship as long as your partner is looking for stability in love. Sometimes, however, you attract someone who is emotionally unavailable, or you find yourself in a codependent situation where you are tasked with helping a lover get their life together. On the path of your own growth, these kind of partners can help you learn how to validate your personality and strengths as the assets they are. As you learn that slowness, logic, and planning are actually what allow you to create the life you desire, you can then attract someone who brings greater balance into your life. A water element would help you get a little bit out of your body and more into your heart, whereas a fire element would give you those little nudges you sometimes need to move outside of your comfort zone. Remember, the opposite isn't always what you desire, but it can be someone who helps you become more of yourself.

Your greatest soul lesson is to recognize that no matter how much you plan for something, you can't ultimately control the outcome. Some of the best moments in life are found by letting go and embracing the divine flow, but for someone who needs to feel they have both feet on the ground at all times, getting caught up in the ethereal romance of love can feel scary. When you can cultivate a sense of inner safety that isn't dependent on external factors, then you tend to make the most of your innate gifts. If everything was taken away — your home, relationship, and financial standing — would you still feel secure in who you are as a soul? Once you master this divine lesson, you will be able to make the most of each moment, even if it's one you never planned for.

Absence of Earth

An absence of earth is one of the most common factors in birth charts, specifically of those who find themselves in karmic relationships. Someone who lacks earth in their chart often lives too much in their head, struggling not just with making plans for the future but also with the basic requirements of day-to-day human existence. When there is an absence of earth, it will be challenging to ground any ideas with real certainty; often the phrase "Get your head out of the clouds" comes to mind with this particular aspect in a birth chart.

The absence of earth means grounding yourself will be especially important, through activities like breath work, yin yoga, or walking around barefoot inside or outside. By physically grounding yourself and getting back into your body, you can bring yourself into a greater sense of balance. This will also enable you to start to work with your strengths, making the most of the elements you do have. Just know that you are going to have to be diligent in planning things out, creating your own sense of stability, and practicing healthy boundaries with others.

Those with no earth placements often find it difficult to put down roots, whether the challenge is in living in one place for very long or in staying in a romantic connection long-term without feeling boxed in. Recognize that this desire to move around is more about trying to create a feeling of safety outside of you because you haven't yet created that feeling inside of yourself. To recognize that you hold the power to create a sense of stability within yourself allows you to then choose situations and relationships based on what you need, rather than what you feel like you're lacking within. Partners with strong air or fire placements can help you embrace more of your inner truth and learn to see your qualities as gifts rather than negatives.

A major soul lesson for you is to stop chasing the next best thing and instead allow yourself to create what you're seeking in your life *inside* of yourself. Try brainstorming and writing down what you've been seeking in relationships, then ask yourself if you've done those things for yourself. A relationship is something that should bring balance to your life, but never what you have neglected to give yourself. You need to learn to slow down, to care for yourself, to bring your attention back to your body. Your task is to recognize that just because you may have to slow down and become more thoughtful to create the life you desire doesn't mean it's impossible.

The Water Element

Water Affirmation: *I am an intuitive, emotional being who embraces my feelings and surrenders to the divine plan for my life.*

Leading Water

When water is your leading element, you lead with your intuition and your heart; you may not see the world logically. You interact with the world around you in a completely different way than others; it's your emotions that decide what you make of your life. It doesn't matter how good something looks on paper — if it doesn't resonate with your soul, then it's not something you will do. You often have an innate sense of justice because your moral compass rests within your heart. You have no problem determining what is meant for you and what isn't. However, because of your deep emotional spectrum and the way that you quite literally feel the world, you can tend to take on other people's emotions or be overly hard on yourself.

In relationships, as a leading water sign, making sure that you have a partner who validates your intuition and is emotionally intelligent will be critical. You may not be the best at making plans and instead will let yourself feel stirred by the phases of the moon, but the more that you accept these parts of yourself, the more you will attract someone who can accept them, too. Life isn't about having to do it all on your own or becoming something that you're not, but instead about owning your strengths.

As a leading water element, you are sensitive and attentive to your partner's emotional needs, and you tend to be romantic. Having a partner who can appreciate your gifts without making you feel less than not only creates balance in the union but also helps you blossom into your full self. You can be more private than most, and even after years together, your partner likely will be mystified that they're still finding out things they didn't know about you.

As you go through the process of your own growth, you'll shift away from personalities who take advantage of your softness and sensitivity, instead gravitating toward those who appreciate all that you are. A leading fire or earth element can help you become more focused, honor your own needs, and continue to progress on your life path. So long as they have the ability to hold emotional space for you with sensitivity, you can cocreate a relationship where you both can be seen and invited to see the world differently. This can ultimately bring in the balance that you seek.

When you embrace your soul lessons as a leading water element, you are honoring your intuition with depth and courage. As you do, you will release the need to prove yourself to others and instead will strengthen your boundaries. To fully honor your emotional realm is so important because it's how you will step into your inner power. Being in your power as a water element means that you feel no desire to make anything be true that naturally isn't. You surrender and allow everything to be precisely what it is, including your own intuitive connection to the divine. When you go with the flow of life, you will attract the love and abundance you have always dreamed of.

Absence of Water

The absence of water doesn't mean that you don't have a great emotional depth, only that you need to cultivate your understanding that this part of you is as important as the rest of you. Having an absence of water signifies that you may take a more pragmatic or logical approach to life, and if you don't have time to feel bad about something, then you don't. Your view of life and relationships might be one of impermanence; you are quick to move on because diving deep into emotions can seem futile or challenging. It doesn't mean that you don't have feelings — you just need to honor them as deeply as you do the other parts of you.

In romantic relationships, having an absence of water can make an emotional connection challenging. Your partner may not feel like you are present for them, like they are special, or like they even matter significantly to you, even though likely none of this is true. It's important to focus on your own emotions and be able to demonstrate to them how you feel. Those with a lack of water can find benefit in journaling using an emotions chart, keeping track of what you felt each day and why. This can help you build up your emotional intelligence and your sensitivity to your partner, especially if you share in that activity with them. It's not that you don't have the emotional capacity to be in a romantic relationship, but that you have to feel safe to be able to explore those softer parts of yourself. If you're looking for a partner, by developing your own emotional intelligence, you can attract a person who will bring balance to your life by stretching your ability to think or act from a more passionate place within yourself, like a leading earth or air sign.

When it comes to your soul lessons, with an absent water element, it's important to create time to reflect on and validate your feelings. In addition, recognize that just because you're fine with how an argument or discussion ended doesn't mean your partner is; sometimes in relationships, it's not just about your perspective but also about being willing to meet your partner's needs. The more space that you can create to feel your own emotions (for example, through meditation, bodywork, or awareness of your feelings), the more you will be able to hold the type of space that you desire in a healthy, balanced partnership.

You Are Whole All on Your Own

With so many different aspects that go into the karmic connection and your own growth, it's no wonder that the karmic relationship is one that truly feels like it inspires you to become your best self. Of course, this is why karmic connections are often confused for twin flames, as there is so much growth potential present in this union. The difference, of course, is that your twin flame will be a constant, an encourager, and will grow together with you, while the opposite is true for those connections of a more karmic nature.

One of the most fascinating aspects of astrology is the study of masculine and feminine elements. Oftentimes traditional astrologers will refer to these as aggressive and passive energies, but that characterization carries negative connotations and suggests outdated stereotypes. The fact is, everything in this world has masculine and feminine energies, even nonbinary or transgender individuals. The phrase *masculine and feminine energies* isn't referring to heteronormative relationships, but merely to the balance of energies that exist within everything in life, including the planets, zodiac signs, and your own personal makeup.

However, I'd like to create some transparency around what the words *masculine* and *feminine* have traditionally represented, because we have to do better at dispelling stereotypes and biases. Feminine energy is not the toxic princess story many of us heard growing up. There is no damsel in distress here, and the feminine is not just about having children and tending to the home. In that same vein, masculine energy isn't aggressive. It doesn't walk around rescuing young maidens, nor does it carry a sword or try to prove its virility through sexual conquests.

Many ideas involving feminine and masculine energies are outdated, particularly in the Western world, where the understanding of these energies has generally been limited to gender stereotypes. This is not what these energies mean in astrology. Rather, your unique configuration of masculine and feminine energies can be likened to parts of you that fuse together to create a totally original self. There are no stereotypes to live up to (or down to). There are no limitations on what you can achieve or how you can show up for your partner. Instead, understanding your masculine and feminine elements simply gives you a new lens into your own truth so you can honor and embody it more deeply.

Clues for Understanding

To know your leading energy is as fundamental as knowing your karmic lesson and your leading element, because it helps you understand your deeper layers and what you need from a relationship to feel like your healthiest, best self. That said, your own and your partner's planetary balance can affect what kind of relationship you desire and what you are able to create. For instance, if you are a trans woman with a leading feminine energy, then you might be seeking out a partner who has greater masculine energy to bring in more balance. Yet, on this path of growth, you may have previously only sought out partners who had a leading feminine energy because of your own path in your gender affirmation.

To discover your masculine and feminine planetary balance, refer back to your astrology chart and look for this section in your reading or count up the number of masculine and feminine planet placements you have using the "Masculine and Feminine Energies" list in the glossary. Whichever has the highest number is what your leading energy is. For instance, the most common balance for anyone regardless of gender or orientation is four masculine and six feminine or six masculine and four feminine. This creates a slight imbalance with the energies, which allows one to take the lead in the decisions you make for your life. Without this, it's almost as if the two energies are battling within yourself over which will take the lead, which creates greater challenges by making you confused about which direction to take in love or even in life. If you have one of these common configurations in which one energy is leading, it actually opens the space for a more profound balance within you, because the leading energy helps direct your life and the choices that you make.

MOST COMMON ENERGY

Masculine	4
Feminine	6
Masculine	6
Feminine	4

Knowing your leading energy allows you to embrace both your strengths and your needs. It also enables you to identify areas you might want to do some work in or bring mindfulness to in order to create a healthy sense of self. You are worthy of love no matter where you are on your journey; however, if you're in a karmic relationship, you have attracted it into your life because a part of you still doesn't know this. As I've said before, the purpose of the karmic connection is not just to help you understand yourself more deeply but also to heal, which will always be the path to your twin flame love.

When you are looking at the makeup of your masculine and feminine planets, obviously it's essential to take note of which is the leading energy, but in some rare cases, there won't be one that dominates — you will instead see five masculine and five feminine planets. In other cases, you or your partner might have eight masculine and two feminine placements or seven feminine and three masculine (as in the charts below). What these energy configurations mean for you will depend on who you are, what type of relationship you are seeking, and what your upbringing has been.

LEADING MASCULINE	
Masculine	8
Feminine	2

LEADING FEMININE	
Masculine	3
Feminine	7

Feminine and Masculine Energies in Astrology

Feminine energy in astrology reflects the ability to receive and surrender, and also an inner strength and wisdom. This understanding rejects the toxic or immature view of feminine energy and instead embraces the all-encompassing divine power that this aspect carries. While the feminine fuels the ability to create, it is not limited to producing children; rather, it shows up in the way that you approach life.

Feminine energy does tend to prioritize emotions, and not only through stereotypical softness: it can take on the fierce, divine powers of Shakti if necessary. Some non-Western cultures, such as the Hindu, have a more developed, deeper understanding of the balance of energies that exist within each of us. Shakti is the feminine goddess who holds the power, the energy, and the life force of the universe. It is sometimes identified as Parvati, Kali, or many other names; in none of these personifications is it a weak, subservient, or vulnerable energy. It is not seen as soft or docile at all. Instead, it represents the divine life force that the world exists through. It is able to protect others from harm.

This is an especially interesting analogy, as the divine feminine is frequently known for having to lead the divine masculine to his heart in twin flame relationships. It's just that we have to put away gender for a bit to see that someone who identifies as male could have a leading divine feminine energy, just as someone who identifies as female could have a leading divine masculine energy. Astrology doesn't depend on your gender or lack of gender identification. It speaks to the energy force within you that will help guide your soul's purpose and your journey into a healthy, amazing forever love.

While the feminine energy receives and brings more attention to emotions, the masculine energy leads or gives forth and is more concentrated on setting up a strong foundation for a life together or navigating the external aspects of our human existence. The masculine energy within each of us is more like that of Shakti's partner, Shiva, who represents the cycle of destruction and creation. This energy sees the importance of having a balanced counterpart, so while Shakti is the life force behind everything, Shiva focuses that force in specific directions, depending on what is needed. Both the masculine and the feminine energies can protect and can also exhibit wrath; they just do it in different ways.

While having a higher level of masculine or feminine energy in your chart will obviously be a strong determinant in your life, cultural conditioning can play a significant role in how those energies play out. We are still learning as a society that men have feelings, too, and have as much of a need to express them, to receive mental health counseling, and to be soft as women have. Your ability to fully receive the energies in your chart is also affected by the conditioning and stereotypes that exist as well as by those opinions or beliefs you have been taught are ultimate truths, although in fact they are merely the perspective of another.

When someone who identifies as female has a greater number of masculine planets, she can tend to make that work to her advantage. Often, women with a significant number of masculine planets — seven or more — would actually come across as more feminine in their mannerisms and appearance, yet they also are frequently extremely successful in whatever business or career avenue they have pursued. Even if as a gender we are still struggling for equality, we have an easier time incorporating different energies within ourselves because we have traditionally been allowed to embrace and express more emotions than men.

For many who identify as female, having a higher number of feminine planets means they have to find balance within themselves in a world that tends to praise the masculine energy and dismiss the creative and nurturing power of femininity. While it's not overtly challenging in romantic relationships for women, having a higher number of feminine planets means that they may spend a portion of their life learning to embrace that rather than being focused on those traits or interests that have been stereotypically labeled as masculine. Ultimately, you are on a journey to release any preconceptions about what any gender should act or look like and instead lean into what feels most comfortable for you as you embrace the power of defining yourself and the life you want to live.

For those individuals who identify as men and have seven or more feminine planets, the results are often quite different, not only because of their potential childhood wounds, but because they have been socially conditioned to have difficulty embracing a multifaceted idea of self. Men who have a large number of feminine placements often develop personality disorders, such as narcissism (something frequently present in karmic connections) or addiction, not necessarily because they aren't capable of embracing the feminine energy within themselves, but because they haven't been taught how to.

However, although there are verifiable reasons why those who identify as men would have a more challenging time integrating the energy of a high level of feminine planets, this is in no way an invitation to try to fix them or help them. In fact, that would be detrimental, because the love and acceptance they need are ultimately those that they receive from themselves. This is such an important thing to know if you are in a karmic relationship with someone who identifies as male and has seven or more feminine planets. Yet rather than it being a rule for all those who identify as men, let it serve as a warning to be aware of possible negative or unhealthy traits that may be present now or surface later on, especially depending on their upbringing and ability to express themselves.

With couples who are trans or nonbinary, this configuration of seven or more feminine planets can affect either partner in challenging ways where it might seem difficult to create a truly healthy relationship.

Ideally, in a relationship, regardless of your identity or whom you are attracted to, the balance simply needs to be that one person has a higher level of masculine energy and one has a higher level of feminine energy. Depending on additional factors, though, it is still possible to have a healthy relationship with other configurations. If, for example, both partners have seven masculine and three feminine placements, but one partner is a leading fire energy and the other is a leading air, then there will still be a balance, because each partner is coming with a different energy that will benefit the connection.

The problem exists if you are craving a more traditional relationship in which you can surrender fully to your partner and have them lead you on important decisions and through life. Regardless of whether this is a heteronormative or a same sex union, the challenge becomes to ensure that the partner you choose has a greater level of masculine energy than you do. Even if it's only by one placement, it makes enough difference to help you achieve the balance and atmosphere that you're seeking in your romantic connection.

Likewise, if you have a strong personality and excel at leading or being in charge of the finances, you will want to select a partner who has more feminine planets than you or with a leading element that would allow you to embrace your strengths without every conversation turning into an argument. In this case, if you both have the same number of feminine planets but you are a leading earth element and your partner is leading water, then you can still create what you're seeking as long as each of you desire to have that type of relationship.

What about when the number of masculine and feminine planets is split right down the middle? At first glance, this might seem to be the ideal, as it brings both energies into balance with each other. However, those with the five and five often have a very different journey of life and love. Yes, they are able to embrace both energies, but until they learn that truth, they will have a challenge doing it with either.

EQUAL ENERGY

Masculine	5
Feminine	5

Interestingly, having five masculine and five feminine planets is becoming increasingly common, especially with children born after the year 2000. Prior to that, the majority of people, especially those who are parents or grandparents now, almost always had one energy higher than the other. Part of the reason for this shift is that society is evolving; we are moving away from the idea of masculine and feminine being a space of polarization and instead are developing an understanding that each individual can incorporate and utilize the different energies that are available to them, regardless of gender identity. But this is something that is just beginning to filter into our world, and so there is a learning curve, as with anything new.

Having five masculine and five feminine planets can often be challenging at first, as you might struggle with how to identify yourself, your needs, or the kind of life and relationship you hope to set up. The elements in your chart can have an influence on your level of difficulty. For instance, if someone with the five and five placement in their chart also has a leading earth element, they will be more grounded and confident in themselves, which will soften the challenge. Largely, however, the five and five is an astrological influence that people need to learn from in order to become the souls they're meant to be in this life.

If you or your partner has balanced masculine and feminine energies, reflect on the healthiness in the connection — specifically, on such qualities as consistency, follow-through, direction, faithfulness, and emotional vulnerability. If there are issues of this nature in the relationship and they have the five and five, then it's likely they are still learning their own balance, and this connection is one that will be more karmic in nature for you.

Again, those who identify as women tend to have an easier time maneuvering and adjusting to the balance of masculine and feminine energies within themselves, just as heterosexual men with the five and five tend to make for very toxic partners. When you break out of the heteronormative relationship, the five and five can still signal challenges, as one has to learn to embrace this configuration of energies. It's something to be mindful of in a partner because, although it's a lesson they are meant to learn, it doesn't guarantee that they will learn it with you or even in this lifetime.

Ultimately, those with five masculines and five feminines are coming into this world to help our planet continue to evolve, to heal the separation and conditioned toxicity produced by our society identifying certain traits as belonging to a specific gender, but it is a journey. And while there are always pioneers who are sent out ahead to pave the way for future generations, you also have to realize it's a process that you can't control.

Those who have the five and five masculine and feminine energies actually hold an immense power within themselves, because they have the ability to choose which to pull from, depending on the situation. It means they will likely have less polarized views on life and will also, with time, be able to embrace more of who they are. However, while that is a strength many of these personalities are learning in this lifetime, it's not reason enough to wait around and hold your breath for a karmic partner to change.

It can be challenging to leave a karmic partner as you come to understand why they are so unbalanced or toxic, but that doesn't mean it's your job to fix them or to accept their behavior, especially if it feels abusive, unhealthy, or as if you have to sacrifice your own needs in order to make them happy. As hard a truth as it can be to hear, the purpose of the karmic relationship is to wake you up to your own personal growth, your healing, and then never to actually manifest into a healthy relationship. The lesson is for you to choose yourself, embrace your self-worth, and be in the position to attract a partner who is in alignment with your divine truth.

Recently a trans woman, Robin, came to me because she had some major concerns about whether her relationship was ever going to become the type of connection that she was seeking. Robin's partner was a man named Kenni, whom she had been with for ten years, off and on. She could see some improvements, which is why she struggled with the decision to end the relationship or to stay.

KENNI	
Masculine	5
Feminine	5
Earth	5
Air	0
Fire	4
Water	1

As we spoke, it seemed that many of Kenni's behaviors were rooted in his astrology chart, not only being a five masculine and five feminine, but also having an absence of air energy. Robin loved him, she could see how he was trying his best at times, but she could also no longer deny his unhealthy behaviors, which revolved around finances and him seeking attention from others. No matter how open Robin was, how loving, how forgiving, Kenni always romanticized what he didn't have instead of tending to their relationship to make it the best they could together.

As she revealed in our conversation, many of the behaviors that would be associated with an absence of air and the balanced masculine and feminine energies in an undeveloped chart had been present in their relationship for a significant period of time. Although Robin said she was confused when we first started speaking, it seemed that ultimately she was looking for validation that the relationship would never actually get better — even if we could logically explain the reasons behind Kenni's behaviors. The goal of healing and growth isn't to remain in a connection that mirrors the wounds of your childhood, but to be able to ascend into one that is better, healthier, and more in alignment with what your healing adult self now requires.

Healing is a multispectral journey. It's not just about learning who you are or tending to your childhood wounds, but also about understanding that everyone has a specific path in life, and sometimes, when things aren't working, you are actually in the process of manifesting the life you are supposed to live — your divine fate.

Evolving into Your Archetype

While the soulmate relationship both finds and leaves you in a space of becoming, the karmic union finds you at your most vulnerable and weak; it is from this point that it can help to shape you into your healing adult self. As you grow and heal, not only does your chart shift from an undeveloped into a developed one, but you also move through different archetypes of the human experience. This movement is essential, especially in the karmic relationship, because it is the way that you reach a new level of maturity that corresponds to your healing and newfound self-worth and autonomy.

Archetypes are universal stages of human behavior and development that help to bring deeper understanding to the choices that are made and experiences in life. These often not only represent stages of growth but also can provide greater clarity in relationships.

Of all the archetypes, the stereotypical ones for women are probably the best known: the maiden, the mother, and the crone. For those who identify as men, the equivalents would be the boy, the man, and the elder. However, I think it's important to introduce more neutral, nonbiased names not only to create a feeling of inclusion for everyone but also to help us realize that sometimes the negative connotations associated with the traditional archetypes can be detrimental to our own healing.

For this purpose, as we delve into the maturity you reach within a karmic connection, I'm going to use the terms *the child* (which corresponds to the boy or maiden), *the healing adult* (or man and mother), and *the wise sage* (the elder or crone). These archetypes are true regardless of our personal experiences (that is, you don't have to literally be a mother to take on your healing adult archetype). They represent important moments of growth.

The whole purpose of the karmic connection is to usher you away from the child and into your healing adult phase. It's the moment that you leave childhood behind and with it the wounds and unhealthy coping mechanisms you acquired. As you fully embrace your sovereignty as a healing adult, you are able to bring your inner child and your inner teenager into a peaceful equilibrium within yourself. On the path of growth, you may have to unbecome what you never were; you may have to outgrow beliefs or ideals that were never yours to begin with; but you should never have to give up parts of yourself, especially those that make you authentically who you are. Instead, this path is about learning how to give each part of you a voice, to ensure that you are working to create a life for your highest good instead of self-sabotaging or excusing away choices that will never lead to the life or love you dream of.

You are all on your own, and you must learn that by welcoming all of who you are — by seeing how your childhood wounds affected what you thought love was, by embracing your inner strengths, by learning from the challenges, and then by rising up on the other side as the person you always knew you were. You just need to take the time to understand that for yourself, because once you do, love will never look the same again.

The Child

When you are in the archetype of the child, you very much have the perspective that a seven-year-old would have toward life. Rarely are things your fault — or, conversely, it seems like everything is. You are looking for attention, the classic "Mom, watch this," except you're doing it with those in your adult life, especially your partner, which can lead to unnecessary drama and conflict. The child hasn't stepped into their power and is looking to be saved, fixed, helped, and loved. Not because as a human they're not worthy of love, but to compensate for what they haven't yet done for themself.

As the child, you have a simplistic view of life and love: "If she really loved me, she would…" You tend to overexplain what it is you want as you try to get your needs met by the very people who will never be able to give that to you. The child cuts people off, erupts into tantrums, and goes off in a sulk when they don't get their way. The child also never assumes any accountability or responsibility.

Many times, if you didn't get to actually be a child when you were young, then this phase is prolonged as you try to get through your romantic relationship what your parents never gave you. The child is the ultimate victim and wants to be rescued. They don't want to have to do anything on their own or make any challenging decisions for themselves.

Instead of looking at why they are choosing an unhealthy or un-reciprocal relationship, someone in the child phase will blame their partner, try to get them to change, or seek others' validation that they deserve so much more by complaining about the relationship to friends. The child tends to lack financial security and the know-how to create a life based on priorities, responsibilities, and desires. They will spend all of their money and then look to others to provide financial support, because in this phase of life they want someone to care for them, in whatever ways they can.

If you date or marry someone in their child phase, the dynamic will look like constant stonewalling or gaslighting, because they lack the skills for healthy communication. They may expect you to handle all the real-life aspects of living together while they do only what they enjoy. A partner in their child phase will refuse to grow or change and

instead will say, "This is just who I am." You might have to constantly remind them to pick their clothes up off the floor or to acknowledge important birthdays in the family. In these types of cases, your partner was attracted to you because you provide the parental figure they wish they'd had growing up. When they rebel against you, argue, or purposely stay out late and turn off their phone, you're also getting to meet their inner teenager.

In relationships, many are operating from within the child phase, because of social conditioning and a lack of growth and autonomy. We are not meant to remain in this phase, but the child can progress only when they are left to figure things out on their own. No amount of love, attention, or financial support will help the child grow into a healing adult. This will happen when they decide that there is a purpose to growth for themselves.

Maturing from the child to the healing adult is a process that happens in phases. Often the karmic lesson becomes a pivotal moment, because that actually coincides with the healing of the inner child. From that point, the mind opens to learning and growing as much as possible; you're starting to see you were never broken or damaged, but only healing.

As much as being in the child phase or engaging in a relationship with someone in their child phase is destined to create an unhealthy dynamic, it is a situation in which you need to practice grace and love. You are never going to grow into your healing adult self if you judge yourself and deny your inner child the love and grace they need. You aren't responsible for turning your partner from a boy into a man, but you are categorically in charge of yourself and your personal healing. Even if it's scary at first, owning up to what is yours to carry, embracing your own growth, and trying to become better for *you* can help you heal the wounds and conditioning of the child and embrace the joy of being your adult self.

The Healing Adult

I am very purposeful in never using the word *healed*, in the past tense, because while a cut on your skin can eventually fully heal, the emotional wounds that we all carry can't be healed as easily, nor are they ever really gone. They can be incorporated differently into your life, and how your triggers react to them can shift, but thinking that somehow you are supposed to reach this state of being fully healed only sets up an unrealistic expectation. The result is we never feel we are good enough.

So I use the term *healing*. You are healing into your adult self, you are healing into your twin flame union, and you are healing into your highest self. But nowhere along the way are you expected to not be triggered by something that hurt you deeply. And this journey of healing isn't about reaching a point of perfection; instead, it's about continually being open to learning and understanding more, which means something you thought you had healed last year may resurface next year for a deeper healing. When you realize that moving away from the child and into the healing adult is a journey, you accept the fact that you will always be imperfectly human while still being committed to showing up and doing your personal best each and every day.

The healing adult is characterized mostly by an increasing level of awareness. They have become the cycle breaker and are learning what it means to love themselves. They've stopped putting partners on pedestals and ceased searching for the parental love they never received, because they've learned to give that to themselves. They have come to understand that whatever they create in life is a reflection of where they are with themselves. They are accountable and try to express themselves clearly.

As you enter the phase of the healing adult, you begin to take greater responsibility for yourself and the role you play in the lives of others; this is really what those traditional archetypes of mother and

man are about. Many people choose not to become parents, but it doesn't mean they will bypass this phase.

The healing adult is someone who is slowly coming into a place of self-worth, of learning what they deserve from life while also embracing their autonomy and practicing healthy executive skills. The phrase *executive skills* refers to the ability to carry out the duties you have in life as an adult human, whether it's getting to work on time, paying your rent or mortgage, scheduling doctors' appointments, or eating healthily. Essentially, it's caring for yourself, which is often inhibited in the child phase, as that is largely about trying to get others to care for you.

In relationships, the healing adult strives for open, honest, and transparent communication. You are able to advocate for your needs, both emotionally and sexually; learning to do that can be a significant turning point, as you become able to say what feels good to you. During this new era of growth, you are still learning, still growing, but you've reached a level that prevents you from slipping back into the childlike ways that kept you in survival mode for so long.

Now, as you begin to blossom into your true self, you start to recognize the power that you have over what you will accept and what you will not. You have healthier boundaries, and you cease participating in arguments with others, trying to prove something. You stop wanting to create a masterpiece out of a work in progress. You allow people to show up just as they are, which changes who you are attracted to in your romantic life. Instead of *hoping* someone will change, you articulate your need and then are fully prepared to walk away if necessary, as the one person you've promised you will never lose again is yourself.

When you've combined learning your karmic lesson, growing into your developed chart, and learning more about who you are, you enter a completely different level of life. This is where you will finally be able to attract all you deserve, because you now know you do. This marks an important change, not just in your romantic relationship, but also in your career, your finances, your spiritual connection, and even your overall life path. As you begin your healing adult phase, it feels like life is finally beginning. Moving beyond the wounds and lessons of your past, you seek to enjoy each moment.

The Wise Sage

The shift from the healing adult into the wise sage is less dramatic than the move from the child into the healing adult. It's a softer transition, and oftentimes, like in the autumn season, you don't even realize this is where you are until you look around and see how beautiful it's all become.

Traditionally these archetypes were seen as age specific: for instance, a woman would be in her maiden phase only until she had children, then she'd be in her mother phase until she entered menopause and left the childbearing years behind. But we are so much more than a body, and as a society we are leaning into our souls more and more. It's becoming clear that you can reach the wise sage phase at any age, just as you could also choose to remain the child in perpetuity if that is where your path leads you.

Personally, I am excited to become a crone and will fully embrace that phase in my life. I dream of the time my waves fall to my waist fully gray, with a crow as a familiar perched on my shoulder. I'll spend my days in the kitchen, growing lavender in my window boxes, making up tonics and elixirs for people in my life, spinning stories around a fire, and delighting in the lines of experience that create intrigue on my face. Unfortunately, though I've been praying for gray hair, it seems I may have to adopt my inner crone before I fully materialize into one, but just because that's a phase I'm excited to enter doesn't mean everyone has to be.

Even as I share about my desire to become a gray-haired crone, similar to the beloved aunts in the Sandra Bullock and Nicole Kidman movie *Practical Magic*, I understand too that each archetype phase has more to do with where you are within yourself mentally, emotionally, and spiritually than it does with anything outside of you. Of course, this is a theme you are seeing come up as you move through the lessons of the karmic connection — as you understand the only thing that really matters is the world you create and tend to within yourself.

The wise sage is outgoing and passionate, far from the stereotypical crone many might dread becoming. But in this phase you have a different attitude when it comes to love. While the healing adult is very action driven, the wise sage is decelerating, taking the time to appreciate life. You're seeing that the highest value is in living a life true to yourself and making time for those who matter most. Perhaps you do this by joining a mountain climbing expedition to Mount Everest, but you may also do it by finally slowing down enough to grow that garden of herbs you've always dreamed of.

The wise sage is completely at home within themselves. When you embody this archetype, you are surrounded by an aura of peace and acceptance, as you realize you don't have to be anything other than yourself. You are less focused on your output than you were in the fast-paced healing adult phase. This means that in relationships, traditional marriage may not matter all that much, and instead it might be enough simply to hold the hand of a partner you know will be there to walk through life with you.

Learning still takes place, since at any age there are new experiences, like children leaving for college or the deaths of those you loved, but it's different now because you've reached a place where you can see the deeper connection between everything in life and your own personal journey. There is a newfound gentle appreciation for all that you encounter as you feel immense gratitude for the process of simply living. Instead of just going through the motions of daily life, you might stop for a moment to have a conversation with the stranger on the corner because you could learn something new or leave a smile behind to brighten the person's day.

In relationships, new connections tend to move quickly, as you are able to discern what is in alignment for you and what isn't, and you hold a great deal of acceptance for yourself and the other person. You tend not to get triggered over small things and instead appreciate yourself and your partner for who you are as individuals.

But the cornerstone of becoming the wise sage is the ability to pass on the wisdom that you have learned through a lifetime of lessons, epiphanies, and forgiveness. In this phase you become the light at the end of the tunnel to younger generations. You are living your life as a testament to who you are and how you grew into the person you've become. While stories are often central to this phase of life, it's also about simply living in a way that can serve as an example to others. You've learned there is no one to impress but yourself and that if anyone is ever lost because you've spoken your truth, then they were never yours to begin with.

The wise sage sets the tone for what will come, serving as a guiding star for those who will come after them. There is an earthy easiness around these individuals, as they radiate the feeling of truly being at home within themselves. They care for themselves, and while they may even get Botox from time to time, they don't sweat the small things. They know they're more than the clothes they wear or the smile lines around their eyes: they are living proof that life is meant to be enjoyed.

Healing Your Childhood Wounds
through the Stars

When I receive a request for an astrology reading, the one disclaimer I mention is that my readings have nothing to do with when you will become rich or get married, as it seems there are countless others out there promising this magic. Instead, I will reveal the pattern of your healing through your birth chart and the charts of your parents, caregivers, and romantic partners.

I first began noticing journeys of growth through the astrology chart when I understood the importance of the placement of Saturn and the South Node in the birth chart. I couldn't believe that other astrologers hadn't discovered it earlier, but then I started to research the patterns of the South Node and the rising sign and saw their significance in the healing journey. Finally, I began including parents' and caregivers' birth charts because to fully understand ourselves, we also have to see the larger picture. It's one thing to want to know when we're going to reach fame or be able to buy a home, but it's another to deeply inquire into how the astrology charts of those who have been poignant in our lives have defined our healing journey.

The purpose of understanding your childhood wounds through the stars isn't just so you gain clarity or confirmation; it can also provide a release. For example, it wasn't your fault you weren't able to have a healthy, loving relationship with your parents as a child — it was destined to be so in the stars. When you look at the astrology and discover why you've always had a challenging relationship with your mother or always attracted a particular type of partner, you realize that there was nothing broken about you, nothing that was wrong or damaged. Rather, these experiences were part of what was written in the stars to help you to learn what you needed to in this lifetime. Such discoveries can be like a salve on those wounds from childhood, because they validate your experiences. They also help you find grace for yourself as you look at how, when you became older, you attracted romantic relationships that mirrored what you had never received or were conditioned to accept.

In one instance, a woman I had been speaking with for five years suddenly asked me to do this type of reading for her. Sierra and I had begun working together after she had what she believed was a twin flame connection come into her life, although she was married to someone else at the time. During our time together, we spoke of childhood emotional neglect and the wound of never feeling chosen. I was excited when she asked me for a karmic lesson reading, because people usually ask when they are ready to learn and to see the truth. And so I gladly compared her chart with those of her parents and of two significant partners.

The first thing I noticed was that both her parents' Venuses were in Virgo, a sign that can have many benefits, but if the individuals aren't progressively learning and becoming better themselves, it can lead to those they love never feeling good enough. In this case, their having Venus in Virgo was part of why Sierra never felt loved, seen, or valued as a child. In her household, affection was predominately a transactional affair, which she earned by doing specific things, such as mowing the lawn or earning high marks in school.

We also found that the gentleman she had believed was a twin flame connection had the same Saturn placement as her — both in Virgo (his chart is on page 140). This meant not only that their connection was karmic in nature as well as carrying the soulmate karmic lesson, but also that Sierra would be tasked with healing the wounds of her childhood through her connection with this man. The purpose of this union wasn't to ultimately come together in romantic bliss, but for her to be triggered enough that she would start giving herself everything she had ever desired in childhood and not received.

SIERRA'S MOTHER	
Sun	Virgo
Moon	Scorpio
Mercury	Libra
Venus	Virgo
Mars	Virgo
Jupiter	Cancer
Saturn	Gemini
Uranus	Gemini
Neptune	Virgo
Pluto	Leo
North Node	Virgo
South Node	Pisces
Rising	Scorpio

SIERRA'S FATHER	
Sun	Scorpio
Moon	Virgo
Mercury	Scorpio
Venus	Virgo
Mars	Leo
Jupiter	Virgo
Saturn	Gemini
Uranus	Gemini
Neptune	Virgo
Pluto	Leo
North Node	Pisces
South Node	Virgo
Rising	Virgo

This is an example of how you can heal yourself through the stars. Those partners you chose who may have betrayed you or caused you pain, or those relationships that never materialized into something more — all were called into your life only to help you heal. You didn't make a mistake in loving them, nor were you ignorant because you tried as hard or for as long as you did. It was just that you needed this type of connection to be able to heal, grow, and evolve into your higher self.

Karmic relationships come into our life to change it, but that doesn't mean these partners are meant to be with our healing adult self. These relationships are built on the premise of childhood wounds. They are windows into what we need within ourselves, mirrors of what we are craving, and catalysts to help us live life as healing adults so that we can attract the real love we have always desired.

SIERRA'S PARTNER	
Sun	Capricorn
Moon	Virgo
Mercury	Capricorn
Venus	Virgo
Mars	Virgo
Jupiter	Virgo
Saturn	Virgo
Uranus	Scorpio
Neptune	Sagittarius
Pluto	Libra
North Node	Virgo
South Node	Pisces
Rising	Aries

Understanding the Patterns

The first step to understanding the patterns that have repeated through your life is a readiness to see the truth. Without this, it will be challenging to fully accept what the genealogical astrology chart will reveal to you; often we need the illusion of the karmic connection because we're not prepared to accept the reality of our third love. To be ready to see the truth means that you probably already have an idea of what this will mean for you. Seeing the truth will serve more as a validation than an epiphany.

To start, you will want to pull up your birth chart, as well as those of your romantic partners and your parents and/or caregivers. I specify caregivers, because in cases where you've been raised by a grandparent, aunt, or nanny, their charts (and not just the biological parents') can affect the patterns in your life. Perhaps this is an argument for the power of nurture rather than nature. Regardless, it shows that everything you go through becomes a part of who you are.

Once you have all of the birth charts, you will want to bring your attention to the placements of Saturn, the South Node, and the rising signs, as well as looking for commonalities where you notice similar zodiac signs. For instance, if your mother passed away at an early age and she had her sun in Taurus, then you might attract partners whose moon, Venus, or Mercury has a strong Taurus placement. This is because there is an unconscious part of you that will be seeking the love and connection you felt you lacked earlier in life. You are looking for the karmic touch points, but you're also seeing if there is a bigger story at play, such as whether all your partners have the same Venus placement or if they have similarities in their rising signs.

As you are looking for the patterns in your partner charts, it's important to also reflect on your relationships from childhood. Perhaps your father was absent, but your mother was always there for you. In this case, you might see more similarities to your father in your romantic partners before your healing began; perhaps you notice that you shifted to attracting more of the energy of your mother's chart in new romantic partners after you started healing.

Be aware that just because there are similarities in the birth chart of a parent and a partner, it doesn't necessarily make the romantic relationship a karmic one. Other important factors include the relationship you had with that parent, the time you attracted the partner into your life, and what it is you are seeking in your life. This is where the need for radical honesty comes in. You have to be transparent — even if only with yourself — about the nature of your relationship with your parent (or caregiver) before you will really be in the place to find the partner connection you need to continue your healing.

My favorite moment in doing readings is when I can see that the individual I am working with has already become the cycle breaker and that they have attracted someone new into their life who breaks the patterns of childhood. For instance, in a reading with a woman named Jaya, I saw that her father's rising sign was Cancer and that every single partner she had — three total — all had Cancer rising as well. In this case Jaya actually had three karmic relationships as she moved through not feeling loved or connected in the ways she had desired in childhood. It was not until she started to face those wounds that she attracted someone different into her life.

As Jaya progressed through her healing, she attracted Aadi, a partner who represented her healing adult self. Until the phase of the healing adult is reached, it's not you who is attracting and engaging in relationships, but your inner child. This is why it's essential to give yourself love and grace through the karmic relationship phase. Even if logically you know what you deserve or want, it's your inner child who is controlling which relationships show up.

In the case of Jaya, when she attracted Aadi she was no longer doing so as her inner child, but instead as her healing adult — hence, the cycle breaker. And while Aadi's chart had similar energy to her mother's, that was actually a positive, because it was an example of what she was taught healthy love was supposed to look like.

Another client, Elsie, reached out to me because she too believed she had come into connection with her twin flame. At first, it seemed perhaps this individual might be her third love, but as we worked together over the years, many similarities between this man and her own childhood emerged. Elsie had experienced childhood emotional neglect, a term that means a child's emotional needs were not meant. It doesn't always have to look like abuse or complete carelessness, but if the parents or caregivers never offered an exchange of "I love yous," physical nurturing, kisses after a scraped knee, or their presence at important school functions, then there is a strong likelihood that the child will feel they never had their emotional needs met.

It turned out that the man she had thought was her twin flame, Ryder, was an alcoholic like both of her parents. When she began to lift the lens of fantasy from the relationship, she was able to see that he ignored many of her emotional needs, just as her parents had. Suddenly it appeared that this connection, which initially seemed to be divine, was in fact one her inner child had attracted.

At the time she met him, she didn't feel of value, and she was looking to be saved from the life she found herself living. Her inner child was triggered and was still seeking validation from this union. While she began to embrace the truth of this connection, it still took her a few years to move through the lesson and purpose of it, something I do strongly advocate for. It's easy to see a client, a friend, or a brother in an unhealthy romantic relationship and say, "Leave them, you deserve so much better." No one can tell you to leave this kind of relationship; the notion that the only way out is through is especially important here. Though Elsie at times felt guilty for staying as long as she did, it was something essential that she needed to do for herself.

Because the purpose, again, of connecting our current relationship to our childhood isn't to just get over it, but to move through it, so that we can learn what we are meant to and never repeat the pattern again.

Had Elsie simply left him because we discovered the repetition of her childhood wounds or because her friends told her she deserved better, inevitably she would have attracted more of the same. Not because that was what she deserved, but because that was what her inner child needed in order to learn. There is always a reason why you are attracting women who mother you, men who are emotionally unavailable, or nonbinary partners who lack the ability to commit — and it's not because it's your fault, but because your inner child is trying to get your attention. It's trying to heal, and it's trying to help you realize that no one's love will make you feel worthy and no one choosing you will ever matter if you haven't first done that for yourself.

The Moment of Healing

In my own journey of love, the one thing that I can say is that it hasn't gone according to plan. I never thought I would find myself crying on the kitchen floor, never thought I would identify as a survivor of domestic abuse, never thought I would get an education in narcissistic abuse when all I had wanted was to love and be loved — yet the universe had other plans for me. And truthfully, if not for the spectacular disaster of my own love life, I never would have started writing or doing the work I do. So there is always a purpose, often not just for ourselves but also for others.

After my first marriage, I thought I was in the best place I'd ever been. I thought I was healed, free, and able to choose a relationship that fit what I really needed from love. However, my inner child had other needs.

When I was about two years old, my biological father had his first psychotic break and was taken to a state hospital, a place no one should have had to be in the 1980s. Eventually he was diagnosed with schizophrenia, and my mother took over the role of raising me solo; for the majority of my childhood, my father didn't know he had a daughter. Logically, I knew he was mentally unable to care for me. I heard the conversations between my grandfather and uncle when they didn't know I was listening, and I was aware that while I sat in a midnight blue station wagon in a parking lot by myself, my mother was visiting my father in the state hospital.

But the thing is, our inner child doesn't know logic. So even though I was aware, had compassion, and spent as much time with my father as I could, it still wasn't enough to heal the wound that had begun to tear at my heart. I felt unloved by my father, not because he left or later passed away, but because mentally, for the majority of my childhood, he thought he was in high school, still playing football and still with his old girlfriend. Having to be introduced to your father each time you see him creates a feeling I wouldn't wish for anyone, especially a child.

In our healing, though, the stars do lead the way. Our charts show us the two aspects of karma we must clear in our lives: the first is personal, through our Saturn placement, and the second is the South Node or our rising sign and the patterns in our chart that we have in common with our partner. After my first marriage ended, I thought I was free to move in a healthy new direction. I attracted a man who was everything that my previous relationship lacked. Diallo never drank. He was quiet and never yelled. He worked hard and was attentive to the women in his life. He sought out time with children and always wanted to talk, showing me that I mattered.

Yet over the next decade, it seemed he became everything I thought I had grown past, and because of his drug abuse, narcissistic qualities, and childlike behavior, I found myself in a similar dynamic to the one I had been in previously. I didn't understand it, until one day I decided to do for myself the chart reading I normally did for others. It goes back to being ready to see the truth, right?

I remember sitting in my car, Ray LaMontagne playing in the background as I waited to pick up my eldest daughter from lacrosse practice. I started simultaneously laughing and crying as I saw that Diallo's chart was almost identical to my biological father's, and, most importantly, their Venus signs were the same. It was obvious that in my relationship with Diallo, I was trying to receive the love I never received from my father, unconsciously believing that then I would finally feel worthy and chosen. But that was never meant to be the outcome.

Oh, Diallo said he loved me quite frequently, but he also would turn to drug use to avoid dealing with challenging situations, and he even speculated that he might be bipolar, depressed, or schizophrenic — yet none of that was enough to serve as a wake-up call. Not because I didn't know I deserved more, but *because it was familiar*. We choose our karmic relationship because it represents a familiarity. Just as Jaya was attracted to men who shared similarities with her father and Elise was attracted to the pattern of alcoholism and neglect, I was attracted to a mentally unhealthy person who had no desire to seek counseling — but instead, karmically, would provide me the space to seek out my own worthiness and love.

I drove home that day feeling on top of the world because I suddenly realized I didn't need Diallo to love or to choose me in order for me to know that I was worthy of receiving that. I spoke to my inner child, I cried, I laughed — and in that moment, I finally felt free.

The Truth Reveals Itself When You're Ready to See It

While in my relationship with Diallo, I believed he had grown into a completely different man when in reality, he had always been that way;

it was just that my wounds, his love bombing, and my need for the fantasy of love prevented me from seeing it. But the truth does reveal itself when it's finally meant to — you just have to be ready to see it.

The karmic relationship is the most challenging to honor the truth of, because every fiber of your being is hoping that it will turn out differently or that it can be changed or healed to become the relationship you desire. But no matter how deep that hope is, there will always be a little voice guiding you forward into truth, and that is what will help you understand how it all served a purpose, even if it was one you never expected.

To understand the truth of the karmic connection, you must be willing to look at how the patterns of your childhood helped determine the person that you attracted. You must come to accept your own imperfections and wounds. And you must realize that just because it didn't work out this time doesn't mean the next one won't in the future. Until you bring healing to your wounds, it can seem like life is bringing you an endless series of romantic challenges, but all it takes is a moment of seeing the truth or of being willing to understand the greater purpose at play, and in that moment you become the very thing you've been seeking from others. You become the cycle breaker. You become the parent and the lover you have always desired. And you look forward to each day, because you know it's going to bring a life that you will get to live on your terms. You know your value rests on the inner worth of your soul, not on anything outside of you, and especially not on having someone else make you feel loved.

The secret with relationships is that while you never need to love yourself first to deserve love, the kind of relationship you attract will be vastly different once you do. If you're starving and hungry, you will likely grab a snack full of sugar from the pantry or stop at the drive-thru for some junk food once again. But if you care for yourself, then you're going to take the time to prepare a meal at home, using fresh, healthy ingredients, and knowing that you are giving your body everything you need.

The thing is, the same is true for love. As long as we're starving for the thing we've always desired and not yet given ourselves, we're going to pick the junk food variety of love. The kind that gives us a bit of a sugar high but leaves us with stomachaches and a feeling of emptiness afterward. But once we see the truth, take our power back, and give ourselves all the love, care, understanding, and nurturing we've ever desired, then we're going to take our time entering into another union. We're going to embrace being happy all on our own first. Only then will we attract someone who is doing the same. And in that moment, we see the difference between the fantasy of love and a love you can put down roots with.

Karmic Relationships Charts
and Journal Prompts

Fill in the blank charts below to create the birth charts for yourself, your partner, and your parents or caregivers. Or you can also download additional charts from my website directly at WordsOfKateRose.com.

NAME:	
Sun	
Moon	
Mercury	
Venus	
Mars	
Jupiter	
Saturn	
Uranus	
Neptune	
Pluto	
North Node	
South Node	
Rising	

NAME:	
Sun	
Moon	
Mercury	
Venus	
Mars	
Jupiter	
Saturn	
Uranus	
Neptune	
Pluto	
North Node	
South Node	
Rising	

NAME:	
Sun	
Moon	
Mercury	
Venus	
Mars	
Jupiter	
Saturn	
Uranus	
Neptune	
Pluto	
North Node	
South Node	
Rising	

NAME:	
Sun	
Moon	
Mercury	
Venus	
Mars	
Jupiter	
Saturn	
Uranus	
Neptune	
Pluto	
North Node	
South Node	
Rising	

Become What You've Been Seeking

While you are contemplating the astrology charts for you, your current partner, and even past partners and parents or caregivers, it will be helpful to notice and reflect on some critical questions.

To identify the personal karma you've been moving through, ask yourself: Are there similarities between your Saturn sign and your partner's? Or perhaps your Saturn is their sun or rising sign?

Are there crossovers from your South Node (which represents generational karma) and your partner's? Specifically, is their North Node in the same sign as your South Node? Or is your South Node sign mirrored in their sun or Venus sign?

Look at your parents' charts and notice if one sign dominates. Does that show up in any of your partners' charts? Look especially for similarities between your parent's and your partners' charts in the rising signs, Venus signs, and Saturn signs.

Can you find the similarities or karmic footprints and see what it was that you were looking for in those past relationships, especially if the energy of one parent or caregiver shows up more often than the other's?

Reflect on whether you were trying to receive or achieve something in your past relationships you didn't have, such as a commitment, faithfulness, or strong communication. Lean into understanding that these relationships were about perpetually having an unmet need. When you can discover what this need was, you will also know how to start healing that wound.

As you're looking at the charts of the significant others in your life and noticing similarities among them, identifying and honoring certain themes, you can also reflect on what were your unmet needs in childhood, even if you would describe your childhood as loving or happy. Perhaps you didn't feel like a priority, or you were made to second-guess your truth. Whatever you didn't receive as a child serves as the blueprint for how to begin reparenting your inner child as a healing adult. The unmet need doesn't have to be large or dramatic, but identifying it gives you the place to start, because giving it first to yourself is how you take your power back. Ask yourself:

What was I trying to receive but never did?
What are the similarities between this relationship and my
    childhood experiences?
Am I trying to receive something, or perhaps trying to help or
    fix a partner, because I felt powerless as a child?

What validation am I seeking through this connection? Lovability, worthiness, value, specialness, et cetera?

Or am I in this relationship because it provides a means of escape, unavailability, or fantasy, so that I can avoid doing work on myself or in areas of my life?

What did this relationship teach me?

Who have I become because of this relationship?

Have I learned to love my inner child and myself as a whole?

Do I know I am worthy, and if so, what makes me feel worthy?

Have I taken or am I taking the steps to create space in my life for what I truly want?

And most of all, do I believe I deserve all I desire?

As you reflect more deeply on your karmic relationship, place your hands on your heart and tell yourself that you are loved, you are worthy, and you are deserving of everything you want and need in your life.

Leaving the soulmate relationship can be scary, because doing so releases you to move into your freedom. Leaving the karmic relationship can be just as difficult, because it asks you to become responsible for yourself and to trust that this connection — which feels amazing — is like that only to keep you attached until you learn the lessons you're meant to.

Find grace and love for yourself for accepting far less than you deserve and for as long as you did. Forgive yourself for thinking that love would ever make you feel less than or as if you had to twist yourself inside out to have your needs fulfilled. Release the idea that you thought love was something that had to be earned, worked for, or bartered with to receive, instead of freely given.

Let yourself accept that just because your karmic partner says they love you doesn't mean it's in the ways that you desire or deserve. Trust that as you follow your healing path forward, you will realize how lucky you are that this connection never materialized into more.

Because, while this is a relationship that is ending, it's also you finally stepping into the self and embracing the life that you were always destined to have, which means you are precisely where you are meant to be in this moment — even if it's a moment that brings you to tears.

When you have learned your karmic lessons, you also will have found true freedom.

Affirmations for the Karmic Relationship

I am able to keep myself safe.

I trust my heart to always lead me toward my greatest healing.

I forgive my karmic partner for all the ways they may have hurt or betrayed me.

I forgive myself for staying as long as I did or for accepting so little.

I forgive my parents for not being present or loving me in the ways I needed when I was a child.

I accept the truth as I am seeing it. I am learning to let that shape a new reality.

I am worthy of being loved in all the ways I desire.

I am capable of healing and creating an amazing life.

I am tending to the needs of my inner child as I learn to give myself what I have always needed.

I can be loved and still not have it be in the ways I deserve or desire.

I don't have to rush through this journey. I need to stay within this moment, reflecting on the truth and letting the universe guide me toward ending this relationship.

I am precisely where I am meant to be.

Everything that I have ever dreamed that love is is real, and I am moving into a place to attract that into my life.

I am creating a life I love for myself.

I honor my truth by continually taking accountability where necessary, practicing forgiveness, and striving to be better each day.

I am whole all on my own.

Moon Rituals for the Karmic Relationship

The moon has always called to humankind because of the vastness that it represents. At times perhaps it reminded us of how big the universe is or how small we are compared to the infinite cosmos. And since the beginning of time, humanity has traditionally used the moon's phases as periods for rituals and to mark moments to honor the cycle of life.

The moon ritual for the karmic relationship emphasizes the healing that has taken place and will continue to unfold even after you've separated from this connection and all that it has represented in your life. This transition must be approached with gentleness.

Unlike the soulmate relationship, it's rare to have the karmic partner remain in your life after separation, not only because of the unhealthy dynamic that is present and will remain so, but because you've outgrown the need for this person to trigger you into healing. There is an old saying (variously attributed to the Buddha, the Chinese philosopher Lao Tzu, or the Theosophists) that states, "When the student is ready, the teacher will appear, but when the lesson has been learned, the teacher is no longer needed."

Your karmic relationship was your teacher. It was never supposed to transform into more. It was never supposed to change. All it was meant to do was teach you about yourself so that you could heal, grow, and eventually attract a healthy, stable, consistent partner — your twin flame, or third love — into your life.

To recognize that the teacher is no longer needed means you are ready to understand that someone else couldn't give you what you were meant to give to yourself all along. In this ritual, then, the focus is on forgiveness, healing, and acceptance.

This is your time to release not just the relationship, or teacher, but the past version of yourself that called this karmic partner in so you could learn your soul lesson. To do that, you have to trust yourself and the new growth that is beginning to bloom like the roses of summer around you. You have to be okay with entering a period of in-between as you close out one cycle and step into the stillness, and the space, from which you will create all you have ever desired.

You went through all you have because you were learning, and now that you have, it's your chance to commit to doing better.

For the karmic relationship, I actually suggest doing both a full and a new moon ritual, because as important as it is to close out the old cycle, it's also important to set an intention for what you want to call in as you embrace the increased power of your healing adult self.

Full-Moon Release Ritual

Start with a full-moon ritual to release your relationship when the moon is in the zodiac sign that your moon, sun, or Venus is in. This will help create a powerful embodiment of what you are moving through and want to let go of, so you aren't carrying anything that no longer serves you.

Once you perform your release ritual, you will want to do your new moon ritual while the moon is in the same zodiac sign. For instance, if your moon sign is in Aquarius, and you do the release ritual when the full moon is in Aquarius (usually in August), then you will perform your new moon ritual with the Aquarius new moon in January.

It doesn't mean that you shouldn't date or open yourself up to new love during that six-month lunation cycle, but after moving beyond your karmic relationship, your main focus should be yourself and creating a life you love. If a new divine love comes in during that time, then embrace it, but if not, don't think you have to go chasing after it either. Healing comes in waves, and it takes time. Knowing that also lets you envision and savor what the next love will fully encompass. You won't ever have to rush something you want to last for a lifetime.

Healing Crystals

Amethyst: This is a protection stone that can help you dispel not only negativity but also any karmic relationship energies that are still lingering. It protects you by acting as a shield while also bringing in a deep sense of purpose and spirituality.

Green Quartz: This quartz brings emotional stability as you begin to transition out of the karmic relationship and into your own power. Separating from your karmic partner can be challenging, no matter where you are in the healing process, and this stone helps you to feel more grounded in your decisions.

Red Jasper: One of the most important requirements when you are releasing this relationship is to know that you are safe to do so. That means you are able to keep yourself safe, you are safe to move on, and you are safe to honor your inner truth. Red jasper helps you embody a feeling of inner safety as you can begin to separate and learn from your karmic relationship.

Jade: This crystal holds the energies of balance, harmony, and abundance; it can also increase strength and luck. As you depart from the karmic relationship, emotional boundaries become incredibly important. Even in physical space you may still leave room for your ex-partner to come back in, or you may become obsessed with checking their social media. Wearing a ring with jade on the middle finger of your left hand can help with this, as the left side of your body represents emotions and your soul, while the middle finger is ruled by Saturn, representing those karmic lessons and the boundaries needed to keep growing through this chapter of your life.

How to Perform the Full-Moon Ritual of Release

Under the full moon, write a letter to your karmic partner, one to your parents or caregivers, and one to the past version of yourself. In these letters, write down everything you have learned from your karmic relationship while expressing forgiveness, acceptance, and peace with all that occurred in your romantic connection and in your childhood.

Most importantly, write down the forgiveness you have for yourself for those choices you made when you were healing, for accepting as little as you did for so long, and for giving someone else the power over how you feel about yourself.

Write this letter to your past self as if you are writing to your inner child. You are ensuring that you are speaking to the part of you that needed to attract this relationship into your life.

As you near the end of your letters, release yourself from this relationship. Release your attachment to the cycle of wounds it represented, the conditioning from childhood that taught you what love should be, and the necessity to go through all you did so you could learn how to truly love yourself.

Once you have finished writing your letters, fold each one three times, folding the paper away from you to send the energy away. Anoint them with rosemary essential oil for healing. Bring the letters and your crystals outside under the light of the full moon and place the letters in a hole in your garden, somewhere where you can burn them safely. Sprinkle in dried rosemary for healing and lavender for peace. Then light the papers on fire while repeating the karmic affirmations that call to you the most.

When the ashes have cooled, cover them with soil from your garden and sprinkle a bit more lavender on top. Depending on the season, you could also plant a lavender shrub here or bulbs that will come up in the springtime, like daffodils, which represent new beginnings.

Place your hands on your heart as you talk gently and with love to your inner child, crying if you need to, because this is an emotional release. Not just for the relationship, but for your childhood and for all of the lessons that you needed to learn to reach this new place on your healing path. Cry and release all that was, all that you learned, and all the ways that you have begun to grow. You are choosing the path of your healing and of transitioning into the adult and higher self, which is the beginning of a brand-new life.

New Moon Intention Ritual

Healing Crystals

Rose Quartz: This is a stone that represents love in its healthiest and best form. It invites in an energy of compassion, romance, and tenderness for all that is to come.

Chrysocolla: As you kindle a new intention for love in your life, both within yourself and in a relationship, peace of mind — which is what this stone represents — becomes essential. Use chrysocolla to emit a frequency of gratitude and a desire to attract only what is meant for you as you are comfortable and joyous in the new life you are creating for yourself.

Amazonite: This is your chance for a renewed outlook on life as you embrace new beginnings. Amazonite helps you feel like you can start over again, not for a second or third chance, but in a totally new frame of mind — as the self you have evolved into because of your healing and growth.

How to Perform the New Moon Ritual of Intention

When the new moon is in the same zodiac sign under which you did your full-moon release ritual, you will focus your energy on what you now want to call into your life. There are usually six months between the time when a full and a new moon occur within the same zodiac sign, so by this point, you have learned to set healthier boundaries and have begun to create a life that truly fulfills your own desires.

In a letter for your intention ritual, write down what you want to call into your life. This letter can be about setting your desires for a new relationship, what type of partner you hope to build a life with, but it can also be about who you want to continue to grow into, what you want to achieve and experience.

In this letter you are committing to creating all you desire for yourself, whether you have a relationship in your life or not. The most important factors are the new standards you are creating for yourself and what you are placing the greatest importance on, because these will become the foundation for whatever you create from this point on.

As you near the end of your letter, speak as if you already have everything that you want in your life and express gratitude for it all. Close your eyes and visualize embodying your intentions, embracing them within your heart and picturing what it will feel like when everything you desire has manifested in your life.

Once you have finished writing your letter, fold it three times toward you, to call your intention in. Anoint it with ylang-ylang essential oil, representing love, confidence, and a connection to the planet Venus, ruler of relationships. When you're ready, take the letter outside with your crystals and, under the darkness of the new moon, bury the letter beneath a rose bush or red tulip or lily, all of which represent love. As you bury your letter, repeat the karmic affirmations for a new beginning that call to you.

When you're finished, sprinkle cinnamon, for luck and abundance, on the earth where you buried your letter, and place your crystals there until the next full moon in the same zodiac sign.

This time, make a sigh of relief and smile. You are healing, you are ready for new love, and you are finally giving yourself everything you've always needed.

Find gratitude for all of the endings you've moved through in your life while you confidently stand up, dust yourself off, and trust that the best is yet to come as you begin to walk into your beautiful new future.

Part Three

THE ASTROLOGY OF
TWIN FLAME RELATIONSHIPS

And so you have arrived at this moment with lessons learned and a hope burning in your heart that it has all been for a purpose — and let me promise you that it has. Twin flames are part of an esoteric legend that is draped in magic and promises complete fulfillment. Traditionally, it was said that twin flames comprise 144,000 souls that were reincarnated on this earth to help teach humanity, offer a higher purpose, and epitomize what unconditional love in the human realm looks like. But that would mean that only 72,000 couples find this kind of love, and in my experience this isn't accurate. I believe we have to widen our perspective. This third phase of relationship can also be called divine love, healthy love, or even, simply put, your third love.

While twin flames have a higher purpose in this lifetime, it doesn't mean that everyone else is damned to a karmic relationship for their entire life. Even if your love doesn't change how the world educates children or doesn't help heal climate change, it doesn't mean you haven't fulfilled your own destiny or that your love is any less powerful.

Truthfully, in many ways I hesitate to use the term *twin flames* anymore. The label seems to have released more unhealthy and toxic behaviors than it has helped to heal, because if someone thinks a partner is their twin flame, they sometimes unconsciously make allowances for that person that they wouldn't for anyone else in their life. But twin flames are real, they are changing our planet, and they are coming together — just like everyone else — by learning their karmic lessons and elevating themselves into a more healed state.

Even if you aren't a twin flame, even if having your relationship serve some higher purpose for humanity isn't on your bucket list, that doesn't mean you won't experience a love that is more amazing than you ever imagined. That's why I expand our discussion to include the healthiest love you can create and call it your divine love, your healthy love, or your third love. Those names still feel as if it was orchestrated by the divine and serves a valuable purpose on your life path — because what you want for your life is just as important as a belief that 144,000 souls returned to earth to help improve our world.

The purpose of your having gone through all that you have was to eventually be able to create the relationship that truly fulfills your needs, that grows out of your healing, and that is there with you each and every day as you traverse the wilds of life. If your biggest joy is simply having quiet moments with your love before you fall asleep at night, no one can say that is any more or less important than what others do or strive to achieve with their relationship. Being able to own the worth of your desires comes down to self-validation and knowing you are deserving of a healthy, aligned, stable relationship — regardless of what you call it.

Many people, if you ask them about their twin flame love, will describe a vicious, toxic cycle of betrayal, abandonment, unreciprocated feelings, and endings. Some may even confess that after their twin flame left, they remained single for eight, ten, twenty years, just waiting for that person to come back into their lives. Yet, as much as they may not want to hear this, that was not their divine love. That is not the healthiest expression of love, nor is that the relationship anyone deserves. And so let us honor the twin flame relationship for what it really is. Recognize the auspicious magic that can surround it, but also ground yourself into reality and embrace that this love isn't going to bring out the worst in you but, instead, your best.

I prefer to use the term *your healthy divine love*. Because this love is the one that was meant for you, it will be the healthiest, and it's also one that's free from any biased labels that have been used to excuse toxic behaviors that actually need to be healed. As Shakespeare wrote, "That which we call a rose / by any other name would smell as sweet." Whatever label you want to use, this love is going to be healthy, supportive, consistent, and able to continue to grow with you.

In all honesty, you can call your relationship a twin flame or not, but it won't change the love you feel, nor will it change its importance in your life. So take back your power and call this love whatever you wish. Let go of the labels entirely; release the idea you have to identify with one and instead just welcome that love into your heart. The love you feel in this connection is the whole reason why you have gone through all you have. You needed to get to the place to accept an easy love, one that you won't have to prove yourself for, to work hard to receive, or to spend evenings up with the moon while composing the perfectly worded text message or figuring out how to change your relationship for the better.

I grew up watching HBO's original *Sex and the City* series and read the book it was based on by Candace Bushnell. I became fascinated, like many of viewers, with the on-and-off-again nature of Carrie and Mr. Big's relationship. It seemed like when Carrie finally received her happy ending in Paris with Big, we all received our happy ending: she was finally chosen, finally loved, and finally told she was the one, so maybe we would get all those things too one day. However, problematically, this storyline actually helped to normalize the romanticism of the emotionally unavailable partner, of holding onto hope that eventually that partner would change and, despite all the red flags, the perfect relationship would come to fruition.

In the spinoff *And Just like That…* on Max, Carrie has to move through the unexpected death of Big in season one, only to be reunited with one of her exes, Aidan, in season two. In a moment of self-reflection, she wonders if Big was actually just her big mistake.

While Carrie and Aidan still end up parting ways, as he decides to prioritize his children, she finally starts to see that perhaps the relationship with Big wasn't all she originally thought it was. As I watched the series, I felt like I was seeing the stories of countless women I've worked with play out on the screen in front of me. There Carrie was, standing in for all of them as they had to face the realization that the person they thought was their great love was actually their great lesson.

Yet even lessons are beautiful, because they mean we are embracing whatever arises with an open and caring mind, all so that we can discover the truth. Just like Carrie, we often have to leave behind what we envisioned a relationship to be or our own idealistic romanticizing of toxicity in order to embrace our inner truth and move into a place to attract the healthy divine love that we are seeking. And that is where you arrive, where you don't have to be anything other than yourself, oddities and all. As long as we are still trying to uphold a certain picture of ourselves or even of what twin flames mean, then we're not open to how love will actually show up. To be yourself in a world that is constantly trying to tell you to be something else is the greatest act not only of rebellion but of self-love.

As simple as it may sound, the fact is that all you have to do is be yourself to attract your great love, your healthy divine partner. Just this. Yet it likely feels as if you have taken a lifetime to learn that there was never anything wrong with you, you were never broken beyond repair, and you were not wrong for the unique way you see life. Love is not found through the clothes you wear, the beauty practices you have, the image you felt you had to create, but by being your messy, imperfect, lovable self.

In a poem titled "Masks," Shel Silverstein describes two people who had blue skin and were searching for their mates, but because they both wore masks, they passed right by each other, never knowing that the other was what they were looking for all along. When it comes to your divine healthy love, this seems the perfect analogy. The moment you remove your mask, you stop pretending to be what you're not or seeking something outside of yourself. This is when you can finally attract someone who has also committed to living life as their full, worthy, authentic self — no mask needed.

It is the moment the healing adult self decides to create a relationship of both love and logic — not to overlook the red flags, but to pay as much attention to the green ones. The moment when the inner child is no longer making the decisions on the basis of their wounds but instead feels satisfied, safe, and loved. And in this space love grows, not from a fantasy that somehow this relationship will solve all of your life problems, but because you know that your partner is as committed to growth, integrity, and truth as you are.

The Difference Is Venus

In the realm of divine healthy love, Venus, the planet of love, becomes incredibly important. Your Venus placement in your chart determines how you love and also how you deserve to be loved. Until this point, though, you were making choices from a lack of something within yourself, so you weren't choosing partners who would love you the way you truly needed to be loved.

Before you claimed your healing adult self, your partner's Venus sign was usually a reflection of the Venus sign of the parent or caregiver who played a part in your phase of wounding. Even if your parent is an incredible person or you can talk about all the nice things they did for you, it doesn't mean that they weren't a reason that you had to heal the wounded parts of yourself that your karmic relationship brought out. If your ex's Venus sign wasn't exactly that of your parent, you will often still find a crossover with your parent's Saturn, South Node, rising sign, or sun sign. A crossover with any of these indicates that you often attract the very thing you felt like you never received or didn't have enough of.

When I received a message from Lucia recently, she said that she didn't know where to turn. She'd been in traditional therapy for years and just couldn't figure out what to do about her marriage; she felt like she was the problem. Lucia felt incredibly guilty because when she looked at the highlights of her marriage — the children, the home, the wealth, the life she and her husband had built — she didn't understand why she wasn't happy. She truly thought there was something wrong with her.

I asked her to send me the birth information for herself, her past partners, and her parents. We can always gain greater understanding when we widen the picture of what we're willing to see. It's with such great anticipation that I set up these charts for a client, because I become excited about what patterns I'll discover and the clarity they can bring. Helping my clients find insights through the charts can make the difference between their thinking they're crazy because they don't feel the way they thought they "should" and truly understanding why they've been feeling as if something was off.

When Lucia first sent over the birthdates, she included those of only two partners. While there was a great deal of karma in each one's chart, it wasn't until we were speaking that she told me the story of a third — her first love. She became engaged in this relationship, which began in her early twenties, but she couldn't get herself to proceed with the wedding plans. Only after her fiancé told her he didn't want to have children did she find the courage to break off the engagement and end the connection.

Immediately, I asked for his information and drew up his chart. It turned out to be the perfect example of Lucia's pattern. Not only had she attracted someone whom she unconsciously hoped would give her what she never received as a child, she had also essentially been dating her father, which made sense given that she never felt emotionally loved or validated by him growing up. This is the importance of Venus and, in Lucia's case, many other placements between her first love's and her father's charts.

When you heal, you change your vibration, and so you attract someone who brings into your life the complementary energy you are seeking. After realizing her own patterns, Lucia was able to attract William, who not only had a complementary Venus sign but also did not repeat the cycle of her father and her other partners. The Venus sign of your healthy divine love will either have the same placement as your Venus; the opposite, which means each other's seventh house of relationships will be highlighted; or placement in a complementary sign. For example, if you have your Venus in Capricorn, you might attract a partner who has their Venus in Capricorn; one who has it in Cancer, which is the opposite sign; or one whose Venus is in another earth sign, like Taurus.

Venus governs not only relationships but also your love language: your Venus sign helps determine how you speak the language of love within your connections. Complementary energy is important, but you don't want it to be so drastically different — like, say, a Venus in Capricorn partnered with a Venus in Aquarius — that it seems you're never on the same page about the relationship nor fulfilling each other's needs. The goal is to attract someone who will understand you, but who through other aspects of their zodiac chart brings enough complementary energy in to create a healthy balance together with you.

Zodiac Love Languages

Earth Signs (Taurus, Virgo, and Capricorn)

As someone with an earth Venus placement, you are most concerned with the stability and functionality of your life. You tend to prefer acts of service when it comes to love, along with planning, which is its own love language. This doesn't mean you don't have a spirit of adventure or romance, but you're going to be motivated to set up your relationship for success. It is important for you to know where the relationship is headed, as well as to ensure that you and your partner are both actively engaged in creating that life. Whether it's trip planning, buying a new home, preparing for a big move, or envisioning your future, you will concentrate on creating a stable foundation for your relationship. For you to feel loved, your relationship needs to be made up of more than just fun dates or promises of what's to come. You actually need to feel the ground beneath your feet so you know it's safe to fall in love and stay in love.

Water Signs (Cancer, Scorpio, and Pisces)

With your Venus in a water sign, romance and feelings are going to take center stage. Spending quality time together; gift giving, as long as it is sentimental; and words of affirmation become the most important themes in your love language. While Venus in a water sign will want an undying commitment in love, it also needs to feel that the relationship is unique and special; because of that, the expression of feelings and romance is essential to your feeling loved. For instance, a water Venus could have their partner plan a trip or take them to look at homes, but if the partner is not providing that expression of love, passion, and devotion, then no matter what they do, the water Venus won't feel truly loved. Conversations, written notes, dates, and sentimental gifts, like the coaster from the restaurant where they went on their first date, are going to pull on the heartstrings of water Venus signs, letting them open up even more deeply to building a love relationship.

Fire Signs (Aries, Leo, and Sagittarius)

Venus fire signs aren't all argumentative or aggressive, despite stereotypes about this placement. Rather, one of the leading commonalities is that they need a balance between freedom and commitment in their relationships. Travel is absolutely a love language spoken readily by this energy, as are words of affirmation, touch, and anything that brings excitement or passion into the relationship, like surprises or doing something for the first time together. Venus fire signs want to experience life, to find freedom, but also to continually know that their person is there for them. It's often thought that these signs have a harder time committing than others, but that is untrue. They actually need a stable place to return to, both physically and emotionally, in order to feel free to be as inquisitive and passionate as they are. The balance of having both roots and wings allows them to always return home, no matter how far they might travel.

Air Signs (Aquarius, Gemini, and Libra)

For those with their Venus in an air sign, conversations are going to be key to establishing and creating a dynamic connection. Air energy rules the mind and communication, so words of affirmation are important for this group, as well as planning and dreaming. Whether by writing or talking, they love to express themselves and to build connection through communication. But they also must know that they are supported in taking action and are being cared for in the ways they need so that they can securely keep reaching for the stars. If your Venus is in an air sign, talking things out and being given the freedom to explore your ideas or new adventures will ensure that you feel emotionally safe. The hardest thing for an air Venus is to excitedly share a new idea with their partner, only to be shut down by the partner saying they don't have time to talk or that it's a ridiculous idea. The more space they have for exploring ideas, talking things through, and sharing emotions, the more a Venus air sign will reveal all their dreams for the relationship they hope to create.

Lovers' Venus Signs

As you've seen, Venus is the planet in astrology that governs our romantic relationships. The most accurate meaning of Venus is that it shows how you love and need to be loved. This knowledge is essential when building a healthy divine love, as you will want a partner to complement your energy while also understanding and validating your basic needs for connection.

The interesting thing about Venus is that, while it does play a significant role in your romantic relationships, it also governs your self-love. How you love yourself is key because, ultimately, it's how you set the tone for all other relationships in your life. For instance, if you have Venus in Pisces, then spirituality and dreaming together become an essential part of a romantic connection. Moreover, your Venus sign will also show you the ways that you should be loving yourself and living your life prior to even meeting your divine partner.

Unlike the soulmate or karmic relationships, in this phase of your life, you are not operating from lack, which means you aren't looking for someone to give you something you haven't already given yourself. In no way does this mean you don't need a partner in your life, but only that you've done the work of making yourself whole, so that you can attract another whole person to become your lifelong partner.

In healthy love unions, you usually have a feeling of meeting the other half of your soul — and while it may feel true in many ways, to completely adopt that perspective is to lay the keys to your own precious locks in the hands of another. In truth, this type of love adds to your life in unimaginable ways; it will be hard to believe you fit together as incredibly as you do. But because, as humans, we believe what we tell ourselves, it's important not to introduce the notion of someone else being your other half into your connection, because you are not half of anything — you are whole all on your own.

Healthy love will make your cup runneth over. It will give you the feeling that you are meeting yourself in another, and that feeling is one to fully embrace, as long as you are defined and clear about who you are and the space that you take up in life. As you've now learned, the reason so many other relationships didn't work out was that you were looking for another to do or be something that you hadn't yet done or been for yourself. Yet as you leave the child behind and enter into the healthy adult phase, you see that you are capable of amazing things. You are able to bring healing to yourself, to create a life of unbridled passion and joy. So when you and your divine partner meet, you can share with your partner that love you already feel for yourself, which is what makes this connection so profound.

To make the break from looking at what isn't healthy to what is, I find myself thinking of a woman I've spoken with off and on for years. When Amara first came to me, she was seeking confirmation that the connection she thought was her twin flame might actually be karmic instead. We worked on what wounds had kept her in that relationship despite her logically knowing it was never going to materialize into more. Those wounds were also what she needed to move through to be in the place to attract her healthy divine love.

I love nothing more than when a client tells me they've met someone completely different from anyone they've ever been with, but with that there is a fear of fully receiving all the goodness. That is usually the sign that the new relationship is the healthy divine love they've been seeking. When Amara messaged me one day, she did so tentatively. She was really excited, she felt completely different in the connection than she had with past connections, but she wanted me to look at the charts to make sure she wasn't repeating any cycles of the past.

AMARA		AIDEN	
Sun	Pisces	Sun	Aries
Moon	Aquarius	Moon	Capricorn
Mercury	Aquarius	Mercury	Aries
Venus	Capricorn	Venus	Taurus
Mars	Libra	Mars	Taurus
Jupiter	Scorpio	Jupiter	Scorpio
Saturn	Libra	Saturn	Scorpio
Uranus	Sagittarius	Uranus	Sagittarius
Neptune	Sagittarius	Neptune	Sagittarius
Pluto	Libra	Pluto	Libra
North Node	Cancer	North Node	Gemini
South Node	Capricorn	South Node	Sagittarius
Rising	Cancer	Rising	Cancer

When I pulled up Amara and Aiden's charts, immediately I could see that instead of the red flags of a karmic relationship, the green flags of a healthy love were present. (Green flags are something we don't spend enough time focusing on. Looking for what is healthy is often more important than narrowing in on what isn't.) In their charts you can see that Amara's Venus is in Capricorn, while her new partner, Aiden, has his Venus in Taurus — both earth signs. This broke Amara's pattern of seeking out partners who had similar placements to her father and also created a complementary energy for the relationship that they would build together. Of course, she didn't know his chart upon bumping into him one fateful afternoon at the dog park, but they were drawn to each other because intuitively they sensed the bond that would keep them together.

Amara was overjoyed and full of gratitude toward me, but I consistently directed her back toward herself: it was her choice to seek help for her anxious attachment pattern, her choice to see the truth, her choice to do the work of healing and eventually to take a new chance on love. There is no set time for how long this process can take, because we are each unique, but as Amara realized she didn't need to have her inner child loved in the ways it had never been because she could do that for herself, she became whole. This was when she started vibrating on the frequency of the very love she was hoping to attract from a partner.

The Golden Age of Hollywood star Loretta Young had it right when she said, "Love isn't something you find" — it's actually something that is already within you. You can't give something to another if you haven't yet achieved that for yourself, whether it's unconditional love, acceptance, or forgiveness. And so, on this journey, you'll find that the very love you've been seeking has been inside of you all along. It's a feeling and an energy that, when uncovered, then attracts the partner and the life you've been dreaming of.

As I said — and it bears repeating — your Venus sign represents not only your astrological love language but also how you need to be loved by yourself. It holds the key to your healing, as it can help you reflect on what you've always needed but perhaps haven't yet received, and then it helps you create the blueprint for how to actually love yourself. It's the connection to self, as well as to the healthy love partnership that was written in the stars for you.

Venus in the Zodiac Signs

Venus in Aries

Venus in Aries takes on a determined and passionate tone. You need your partner to stand up to you, because you are attracted to strength, but you also want them to trust your opinion and support your dreams. As an Aries Venus sign, to be successful in love you have to own who you are. Healthy debating with your partner can be an important part of your connection, but you can't spend each and every moment of your life fighting, either. Having a partner who is softer, who can compromise or seek out the direction you provide, will make for a healthier dynamic. Because you want your partner to appreciate the way you approach life, you thrive with words of affirmation. By the same token, compliments make you feel your partner understands that everything you're doing is for the good of both of you.

In love you tend to go after what you want, but you may need to learn to appreciate what you have, too. The thrill is not necessarily in the chase but in the connection. Be wary of starting arguments for excitement; instead, create time for new experiences with your lover. You need to feel like there is always something new to learn, and doing this together can help prevent unintended arguments later. You have an enormous amount of love to share with your partner, and you bring a passion for life that is positively contagious. You just need to first set yourself free from any obligations or preconceived notions of life before truly committing, so you really will be able to build the relationship that fits your unique desires.

Most Complementary Venus Signs: Leo, Libra, and Aries

Venus in Taurus

Taurus is one of Venus's home sign placements, so your Venus is extraordinarily strong if it is in Taurus. Venus in Taurus needs a solid relationship full of joy. You often express your love by creating a luxurious home for you and your partner to live in — not luxurious in a superficial way, but in a way that feels genuinely good for the soul. You also love gift giving, as it represents not just the item itself but the intent and thought behind it. As a Taurus, you do not do well with struggle, and so you need a romantic connection that feels natural and develops organically. Be wary of being overly stubborn or dictatorial in your relationships, because such behavior can suffocate the connection and end up harming the love you want to receive and give. Because of this need for compromise, it is essential to stick to what you know you need while remaining flexible around how you want to receive it.

Having a partner who enjoys how you beautify yourself and your home is essential, but try to remember that money and material items never equal love. While a Venus in Taurus often needs to learn that it's not things that add value to life, but true connection, you also offer a very stable and grounded approach to love. Having a beautiful life is important to you; more important is to create one that is thought out and built to increase stability and strength. Situationships usually only cause anxiety, as they present too many unknowns, so make sure that as you approach the divine healthy love, you are truly honoring what you need from a relationship. Compromise is key, but so is knowing what your personal nonnegotiable is as well.

Most Complementary Venus Signs: Taurus, Cancer, and Libra

Venus in Gemini

With your Venus in one of the two signs of the zodiac with a sense of duality (the other being Pisces), it is crucial to know who you are before entering a relationship. This duality can be seen as the human and the soul and also as the wounded and the higher self. The human can become distracted by a passing fancy, while the soul will always remain committed to what it knows is divinely fated. Knowledge of how this sense of duality shows up in you will help minimize the arguments and the ways you may unconsciously change yourself to make a relationship work — especially if it's not meant to.

Gemini is also the Venus placement most known for having a wandering eye, which implies a potential for affairs or, at the very least, an inability to fully commit. Being rooted in who you are will help you choose someone who complements you instead of feeling as if you or your partner is constantly adjusting to changing whims. As an air sign, for you conversations are key, but they need to be more than entertaining; they must contain the depth you need to build a strong connection. Words of affirmation can be vital for you to feel genuinely appreciated for who you are, as can receiving gifts from your partner, which can instill a sense of specialness and devotion.

As a Gemini, you need to feel engaged with your relationship, especially if you're to remain committed instead of trying to have your needs met elsewhere. An important part of this is knowing what you need from your partner and your relationship. By taking the time to fully embrace all the different sides of yourself, you will attract a partner who will do the same. Let go of any worry that being yourself is fraught with contradiction and instead simply accept yourself as you are. You don't need to be anyone other than who you are to deserve the love you seek, but you do need to ensure you're investing your energy in a connection that you genuinely can see yourself growing with.

Most Complementary Venus Signs: Gemini, Sagittarius, and Aquarius

Venus in Cancer

Home and family are essential when you have Venus in this water sign. Ensure you are honoring these needs and not trying to play it casual in relationships, because otherwise, no matter how much love you might feel you're getting, it won't be enough. Satisfaction within your home is key to your overall well-being. Whether you have an apartment for two or a house for your family, this satisfaction will determine how fulfilled you are in your relationship and even your life in general. If you decide to have children, nurture the connection with your partner first and foremost. Do not let it become all about the family, or your relationship may suffer; you often have to learn that you can't abandon yourself in the process of loving others. This is an important lesson that frequently arises in the karmic relationship, so that as you enter the healthy divine love phase, you are able to find greater balance.

Stability is essential to you, but remaining quiet to keep the peace is never worth it. Once you learn that all of your feelings and needs are valid, you can then attract someone who will reflect that back to you. A partner who can hold space for you and your emotions is vital, instead of a dismissive partner who may chalk your feelings up to moodiness. This feeling of emotional safety in your relationship will bring the depth of connection you desire.

Quality time with your partner is especially important, but rather than doing exciting things, focus on enjoying those quiet moments at home together. As a Venus in Cancer, one of your more important tasks is to make sure you have activities and pursuits outside of your home and family that bring a sense of validation. This is one of the most loving and devoted zodiac signs for Venus to reside within, but make sure you are also honoring your dreams and goals for your life.

Most Complementary Venus Signs: Taurus, Cancer, and Pisces

Venus in Leo

If you have Venus in Leo, being your partner's top priority is essential for you to feel like the relationship is satisfying. Your sign is known for following their heart — a huge asset, as you will not let anything stand in the way of you and the person you love. However, it also requires you to follow your truth rather than simply falling into an infatuation. Venus in Leo can be so tuned into their heart that they forget there's a difference between a momentary attraction and a lifelong partner. Taking time to reflect on your feelings prior to entering into a committed relationship can help ensure that it is one you will resonate with for years to come. Physical attractiveness is huge for you, but remember that it is not how you look together as a couple that matters, but how healthy your bond is behind closed doors. You have a deep capacity for love and passion, but understanding that how it feels is more important than how it looks is something you will have to learn in order to attract the kind of relationship you seek.

Having a partner who goes to great lengths to make you feel special, seen, and heard is essential for you to feel like you are loved. If you lack that, you have the potential to act out dramatically — giving them the silent treatment, making them jealous, or indulging in emotional outbursts. All of these tendencies can be positively dealt with after you grow out of the child phase, but you still need to remain aware of them, because you and your partner should never feel like you're in opposition — you want to be part of the same team. Asking for those important words of affirmation or for quality time to share what you need will help you feel that you are one of their priorities. Make sure you speak about your needs instead of just reacting. Practicing a pause in the moments when you feel reactive will make all the difference, not just for your relationship but for your own healing journey.

Most Complementary Venus Signs: Leo, Libra, and Scorpio

Venus in Virgo

Virgo is a challenging placement for Venus. While Virgo does not have a wandering eye like Gemini, it often needs perfection. Idealistic ideas of love can prevent you from attaining fulfillment in relationships.

Recognize that even in a relationship, your partner is their own person. Be clear about your needs, but take time to notice where they are making an effort rather than whether their actions match the picture you had envisioned. As a Venus in Virgo, you frequently have very specific notions of what a relationship or even life with a partner will look like; the lesson here is that the more you release those ideas, the more you will attract what you desire. A mindset of gratitude is essential in relationships, because you can tend to look for what's next or what isn't occurring more than what is. By focusing on what you are grateful for, you can actually inspire your partner to show up even more fully.

Virgo is a healing sign, so taking on partners you then try to fix may be alluring, but remain mindful not to be dating someone's potential rather than their reality. This tendency can show up as codependency or simply as wanting to be helpful to someone that you love, but either way, you have to see your partner as who they are instead of who you think they can become. Accepting this reality can save you a lifetime of heartbreak.

For you, one of the most important aspects of love is being able to grow together in a way that feels aligned and enriching. Growth as a couple means you can hold space for your partner to grow on their own while you feel confident that healthy space is essential for love. This only adds to the overall strength of the connection. Spending quality time together or doing acts of service for each other enables you to feel loved by your partner and to feel that the energy invested is reciprocal. Stay clear on what you need, and appreciate when those needs are being fulfilled rather than constantly raising the bar. Continually pushing for perfection will make your partner feel like no matter what they do, it is never enough — even when you are actually feeling satisfied by the connection.

Most Complementary Venus Signs: Cancer, Pisces, and Virgo

Venus in Libra

Libra is the other ruling sign of Venus, but Venus operates differently here than in Taurus. Libra is the sign of balanced reciprocal partnerships, which means that this kind of relationship is essential for you. Love becomes practical here through acts of service or other means. Part of your inner work is being direct and clear about your emotional or real-world needs, which helps your partner know how you need to be loved. Remember, in relationships, balance is not to be found in making everything fifty-fifty but in each person's ability to complement the other and to show up as best they can each day. Stay mindful of the energy you pour into a partnership, because while you may expect to get it back, it will drain you if you don't. Learning to create space for your partner to step into is crucial for you to find the balance you seek. If you're the only one planning dates or thinking about how to progress the union, you'll likely feel unfulfilled. The way to remedy that is to create the space for your partner to take the lead sometimes — and then trusting that they will.

As a Venus in Libra, you tend to shy away from arguments. Forever the diplomat, you believe in talking things through and finding a solution that works well for everyone involved. When it comes to love, being with someone who can provide direction can be of benefit, as long as you are also doing the work of sharing your innermost feelings. As a Venus in Libra, you often choose to sacrifice your inner peace in order to keep the peace in your relationship, but as you no doubt already have learned, this never works. Let yourself have hard conversations and open up to your partner, as that is the only way to create that sense of genuine partnership that you seek.

Most Complementary Venus Signs: Aries, Taurus, and Libra

Venus in Scorpio

Scorpio is a deeply passionate placement for Venus and one that takes some time to become accustomed to so that you can learn how to use this energy to your advantage. Sexual chemistry and connection are essential for you in relationships — something you need to embrace instead of repress. Physical touch is one of your primary love languages, but it's not just about sex. Rather, it gives you the ability to intimately connect with your partner, because you desire not just a relationship but the feeling of merging souls. Having deep emotional conversations is another good form of connection for you, but to have this you must be comfortable with your truth, which is a product of your personal growth. Someone with Venus in Scorpio often keeps secrets — whether they're of an illicit nature or just the truth of your feelings — which affects a relationship's overall connectivity and longevity. Knowing your truth before committing can help you be more transparent with your partner, allowing you to be honest about your needs.

When it comes to love, you aren't just looking for a relationship, but for a special, unique connection that is found only once in a lifetime. You want depth, magic, and intimacy. Oftentimes Venus in Scorpio can stay far longer than is beneficial in romantic connections that are karmic in nature purely because of this desire to have something that feels otherworldly — even if ultimately it doesn't feel healthy. As well as ruling over the darkness and secrets, Scorpio also rules the occult. As I mentioned, you have a strong desire to merge with your divine counterpart, but you if you act on this, you need to make sure you're coming from the stage of the healing adult, so you don't end up spending decades in your karmic relationship. You want your lover to be deeply committed to you, because this helps you to feel secure, but learn the difference between connection and obsession. As you grow within your healing, you can leave behind jealousy and possessiveness, instead feeling content and trusting in the unique soul connection you've been able to build.

Most Complementary Venus Signs: Leo, Scorpio, and Pisces

Venus in Sagittarius

The Venus in Sagittarius placement may impel you to wander in search of experiences of the soul. This impulse has nothing to do with an inability to commit but instead is propelled by the desire to find someone to explore life with. You are always searching for a relationship with solid roots that also encourages you to fly free. The more secure you are in your relationship and the greater the loyalty and presence of your partner, the more you feel you can explore life. While you are likely to create a new relationship paradigm that satisfies your own desires for love, it doesn't mean you won't commit — you just need to feel that a relationship isn't making you give up the best parts of life but instead is making you able to embrace them.

You are known for being a seeker of truth, but you can also get distracted by everything else; you will discover that it's your journey to your own inner truth that is most beneficial for you. Sometimes the greatest horizon to explore isn't in another relationship or a far-off country, but the one within yourself or even in your home. You can delight in learning and experiencing new things with your partner as you incorporate your quest of exploration into your connection. Whether traveling to exotic destinations or trying some new pursuit like yoga, you need to feel that stimulation you get from spending quality time together enjoying and exploring life.

Intelligence is a massive factor in attraction for you, as you are known for being one of the most philosophical signs of the zodiac. Take time to engage in deep conversations with your partner to help expand your connection. As long as you don't sweep anything under the rug, address any issues or feelings as they arise, and never forget the value your partner brings to your life, you will continue to grow the love of your dreams.

Most Complementary Venus Signs: Gemini, Sagittarius, and Aquarius

Venus in Capricorn

Capricorn is one of the zodiac's most committed and loyal signs. Casual relationships will not bring the feeling of stability Venus in Capricorn needs from a partner, even if you share a great depth of love. You might even be a serial monogamist, preferring long, serious relationships over the experience of dating multiple people, as it can be hard to feel like you have to divide your energy up among various lovers. Capricorn is an earth sign but also highly ambitious, so having the same sense of drive as your partner is essential, even if it's in different areas of interest. While it's not specifically about your partner's career or other endeavors, you are attracted to ambition and drive because you want to create both a successful relationship and a successful life. This is in part due to the stability earth signs are known for, but also you have a desire for each person to be able to accomplish their dreams. To feel most loved, receiving words of affirmation, acts of service, and planning from your partner can be of benefit, as it's not just the romance that you desire but the feeling of fully supporting each other in creating success and abundance.

Because you are incredibly loyal, you tend to keep your head down in unhealthy or unfulfilling relationships and keep trudging ahead far longer than is necessary. In relationships, don't stay together just because it seems the easiest path to take or because you've been together for numerous years already. Find the courage to heal any unhealthy tendencies so that your partner doesn't become an encumbrance holding you back from living your best life. Starting over is not the worst-case scenario — hoping that your needs will be fulfilled by someone who is not right for you in the long term is. You are looking for a forever love who is also a true-life partner, because for you it's not just about the relationship but about what you can cocreate through your love for each other.

Most Complementary Venus Signs: Capricorn, Cancer, and Pisces

Venus in Aquarius

Venus in Aquarius is a very independent placement; you must feel like your own person, even in the most committed relationship. Recognizing what works for you instead of following a blueprint of what relationships are "supposed" to be like will be an essential part of your journey. You are known as the rebel of the zodiac, which means you may gravitate toward the untraditional rather than following any prescribed relationship to-do list. You are meant to be someone who sets a new precedent for love as you embrace the magic that can exist when you welcome your full, authentic self. When it comes to love, don't ever try to fit yourself or your partner into a box. As much as you like to feel free to do life on your terms, you can sometimes neglect to give your partner the same leeway, yet you will find that when you do, you truly can create the relationship you have always desired.

It's essential to validate your needs for personal space or alone time in a connection. The right partner will support you in that and benefit from it, instead of feeling hurt because you want to spend an evening by yourself. Alone time is something you need so that you can check in with yourself about your feelings or your dreams for your life.

Being able to embrace spontaneity in a relationship is vital for you, so quality time becomes an essential kind of love language, as does performing acts of service to balance out your overly independent nature.

Be mindful that a fine line exists between healthy autonomy and hyperindependence that stems from wounding, because you do not trust others to show up for you. In a connection, allow your partner to be there for you and support you. Just because you can do everything yourself does not mean you always have to or that you should. In letting someone step in to help you, you also create the space for your lover to feel like you trust them and value their presence in your life.

Most Complementary Venus Signs: Gemini, Sagittarius, and Aquarius

Venus in Pisces

While not one of the ruling signs of Venus, the planet of love does exceptionally well in Pisces, the zodiac sign that represents unconditional love. This water sign loves romance, so meaningful gift giving, quality time together, and physical touch are incredibly important to help you feel connected and nurtured. As I mentioned earlier, Pisces is one of the two signs in the zodiac that holds a sense of duality, the other being Gemini. While Gemini represents the human and the soul, the duality of Pisces (depicted as two fish swimming in opposite directions) represents the conscious and the unconscious mind. It's no surprise that this sign carries a great need for depth, but it also requires a lens of truth, because a great deal can lurk within the unconscious. As the twelfth sign of the zodiac, Pisces is known for picking up traits from the other eleven signs and for being the most connected to the spiritual realm. Having an emotionally mature and open-minded partner becomes crucial if you want to build a relationship that lasts.

Oftentimes, one of the lessons you must learn is to not become overwhelmed by your feelings but instead to hold space for them without becoming fearful or anxious. As loving and magical as Pisces is, those with Venus in this sign also can tend toward escapism or seeing things through rose-colored glasses instead of what is real. Yet when you can swim in your own ocean of duality and find peace, you will be able to attract a partner who holds space for you and helps you to ground your deeply spiritual ways. As the perpetual romantic, it's important you are not fixated on a romance-novel type of love; you need to appreciate all the ways your partner is trying to show up for you in real life. Focus on creating a union of patience and understanding with someone who can help ground you in the reality of love instead of staying in the clouds, dreaming of what you think love could be like.

Most Complementary Venus Signs: Scorpio, Capricorn, and Pisces

The Fate of the North Node

No matter where you are in your journey of healing or of love, it doesn't change the fate that was written in the stars for you. After heartbreak, loss, or the shock of reality that can come from entering the phase of the healing adult, so often it can seem as if love no longer gets to be magical. Your perception of love changes as you start to see it from a healthier point of view. But in the same way that you let your eyes adjust to the light after walking through the darkness for a long time, you will eventually realize that the healthiest love is also in fact the one that is most magical and divine.

Instead of seeing unavailability or avoidance as exciting or alluring, you start being turned on by consistency, accountability, and open communication. As much as your younger self might never have believed it, what is the best for you can also be the most amazing expression of love that you could ever have imagined.

The secret to all this rests in the North Node. Just like the South Node, the North Node isn't a planet at all, but a mathematical point on the moon's orbital path that governs the cycle of eclipses. The location of each node at any moment in time will govern what zodiac sign the eclipses are in, and for you it also decides your fate. While the South Node rules over your personal karma from previous lifetimes, as we discussed, the North Node oversees your fate, what was written for you in your soul contract. This is the life and love that you are forever being guided toward, even as you move through the lessons of your past. However, there's one important factor to know when working with the North Node: the fate it governs is never a given, but has to be chosen.

Many times, when I'm speaking with clients, they will adopt a lackadaisical approach to their fate, saying, "Well, if it's meant for me, then no matter what I do, it will still be mine." At certain points this is true: what is meant for you always is, and you are given different opportunities to learn, grow, and then choose your fate. However, as much as destiny is always at play, so too is free will. If fate really was guaranteed no matter what you did, then you would never have to learn the lessons that enable you to consciously choose it. It would fall into your lap in the middle of a karmic relationship or find you when you were consistently making unhealthy choices. But such scenarios go against the very nature of the North Node.

While the lessons of the South Node are yours whether you choose them or not, the fate and abundance of the North Node have to be earned. To be in alignment with your soul, the North Node asks you to make the hard decisions, to learn the tough lessons, and to be willing to release all you thought life and love were so that you can welcome in what is meant for you. And so the North Node works benevolently — just as all of the universe does — but its gifts have to be consciously chosen after you learn the lessons of the South Node.

Everything in life is preparing you for the next steps in your journey. In embracing the lessons and growth offered by your karmic relationship, you have shown a willingness to expand beyond your wounds, and you are now primed to consciously choose your fate. When I speak with people who are actually in their karmic relationship — especially those who have been married for a significant period of time — and I reveal that to them, they inevitably ask me, "So does that mean I have to get divorced?" And my answer is always the same: "No, of course not. You don't have to get divorced" — but I always let them know that the relationship will never improve beyond where it is right now; it will never shift into something that brings true fulfillment, happiness, and love; and in that moment it is the best it will ever get. No one should ever feel pressure to get divorced, to separate, or to make any other big life decisions, but with that has to come the acceptance that the relationship they are in will never become what they truly desire.

No one has to choose to embrace the fate of their North Node, but it is a divine gift that is available. So many times, we forget how amazing it is that we are being fully supported by the universe in all we do and that we are always being given a choice over who we will become, what life we will live, and what relationship we will commit to. And each choice matters. Just because the universe will continue to offer a spiral of events returning you to important themes and lessons doesn't mean it's permission to bypass what you know is meant for you simply because you don't feel ready to choose it — or you're betting on it always being an option.

In certain situations, there is the option to completely ignore your fate and choose a different path. But to ignore the fate of your North Node means you are choosing a more difficult path, not just for love, but for life itself: you are showing the universe that you need more lessons in this lifetime. It may not mean that each day is wrought with pain or sadness, but you are choosing on the basis of what you want as a human, not necessarily what your soul is longing for — what it was born to create and live. In that choice, you are separating from your soul.

You have to practice care when making decisions in your life, especially when it comes to your healthy divine love. Although it was written in the stars and what was meant for you will always divinely be so, it is your choice whether to choose it or to remain where you are. Just realize that to remain in anything you intuitively know isn't meant for you — whether it's a relationship or a life situation — is to vibrate on the frequency of needing soul lessons. But when you choose the path you know in your heart you're meant to take, the entire universe conspires to help you.

And so, in embracing the fate of the North Node, you are drawn to the person that you signed your soul contract with. The one who was meant to join you in your healing, not your wounding. The one who will be a part of your blessings and not the pain in your lessons. It is the beginning point, not just for the love you imagined might exist, but for the life that has been waiting for you to finally arrive.

When Your Human Meets Your Soul

The significance of the North Node with regard to your healthy divine love is that you share the same destiny, the same fate. In this relationship, it's not just about finding someone who is compatible with you but about being with a partner who truly fulfills your soul path. And the irony is that this isn't something you can find at all, but a relationship that finds you. Rarely does anyone go looking for this type of relationship; instead, it seems to be one that appears suddenly from nowhere or else a connection that is already in your life as a friend or acquaintance and you suddenly wake to the reality that this is your healthy divine love.

While your inner child or teenager has been governing your romantic decisions up to this point, now it is your healing adult self who's running the show. As you embrace your healing and growth and find that you are happy and satisfied with who you are in this moment, that is when this relationship begins to form in your life, because you are finally radiating the energy of wholeness on your own.

Many times, the person who ends up being a forever love is one who has already been in your life. It's someone who perhaps you've remained in contact with or share an inexplicable bond with as you've each gone through your journeys. While what I'm describing is more often associated specifically with twin flame relationships, the idea of your person already being in your life or, if you've just met, feeling like you've known each other is a common one in these unions. This phenomenon comes from the North Node.

Having moved through all you've had to in your life to reach this point means you quite literally aren't the same person you used to be. No longer are you struggling to feel worthy, trying to give your inner child all they need and never got, or clinging to a relationship out of fear of being alone. Instead, you have come home to yourself. You have realized that you were the one you'd been searching for this whole time. And because of that, you're in the position to see what love really is.

When I am speaking with clients, it's not uncommon for them to mention that this amazing healthy relationship they have is with someone they would never have suspected they'd be with. This partner breaks all of the molds for what they'd previously thought was love; it can take a bit of time and effort to work through the acceptance of it. Yet no matter how disorienting the relationship might be, it exerts a pull that continues to draw you in, even if you are still growing through the lessons necessary to get you to the place to receive it.

In one of my favorite stories, a woman I've spoken with for close to a decade, Ingrid, called me aghast because she couldn't believe what the man she was dating did. I anticipated hearing the worst, only to hear her say, "He picked me up in a boat for our date, Kate! He picked me up in a boat, complete with picnic and sunset!" I started laughing, because it's ironic how when we start to receive the very thing we've always desired, it can seem unbelievable or cause us to question if it's real or not.

I am glad to report that Ingrid and her partner, Harry, are still happily together today. And while the relationship has a great deal of magic and connection, its importance has actually been more about their own healing and ability to receive the kind of love they've always desired. These relationships don't just automatically work because they're destined to or even because of the North Node, but because each person consciously chooses the other and resolves within themselves to approach love and relationships differently than they did before.

Yet the connection is subject to the draw of the stars. Even during moments of challenge, which are often the product of growing pains, you may feel continually guided toward each other and the life that for each of you is destined and was always so, long before you entered this life. To believe in true love, in magic, in fate is also to be able to understand what love truly is.

This is the difference between the karmic and the divine healthy love relationship. In the karmic connection, we think that the conversations, the sex, the way we can't stay apart all mean that we are meant to be together — regardless of whether one or both of us are married or how unhealthy the relationship might be. We justify the toxicity by defining it as the magic, as the divine connection we want to believe in. But healthy divine love comes differently. It comes with growth, with awareness, with being able to make the morally right decision even if it's not what your heart is longing to do. And in the process, you start to see that the real magic is the ability to bring out each other's best selves and to consciously choose a life together, no matter where each of you may be individually.

This is the union that helps introduce you to your soul. Not because this partner is necessarily your other half — after all, we are all whole — but because it's someone who honors you for being your true self. To be truly loved is also to be with someone who will make the hard decisions if it means honoring who you are and what you are worth. You can go through a spiritual awakening all on your own, and likely it's the karmic relationship that begins this process, but because as humans we need connection with and confirmation by another, it's your healthy divine love that mirrors who you've grown into. In this relationship, your partner encourages you to go more deeply into your soul, because they love, value, and appreciate all that you are. You don't need to engage with your reckless teenager to get their attention or plead from your inner child to receive love. Instead, attention and love are freely offered, whether you are at your best or your worst.

When your healthy divine love shows up in your life with their only desire being to love you, to be there for you, and to share as many amazing moments as you can together, it registers as permission for you to be as wild, unique, or transparently authentic as you can be. A healing is taking place, but instead of it being your inner child trying to be loved, it is your healing adult feeling confirmation that you were never too much to love, show up for, or be chosen. It's seeing reflected in another what you've already given yourself, what you've begun to accept and grow in your life, yet when suddenly another begins to do that for you, it becomes the love you have always desired and deserved but never received.

The idea of twin flames is charged with mystery; we all want our love to be unique. We want our relationship to be destined in the stars, to be fated, and to be so very special, because life is mundane enough and love, in its best form, should be magical. But to be the product of true magic, it also has to be healthy, it has to bring out your best, and it has to meet you in healing too. You are deserving of a love that defies logic or time. No matter how old you are, when this type of love sneaks in, you will feel in many ways that it's the first time you've ever loved, because you've finally learned what that actually is.

The Value of a Relationship

When it comes to your healthy divine love, there are five factors that keep it together no matter what you might be going through. These are rarely, if at all, present in any other connection, which is what makes this one so powerful. Just because two people stay together doesn't make it a relationship that is the highest expression of love. That's determined by whether or not these qualities are present within the connection, because it's not just who you love but how you love that makes all the difference. Let's look at the feeling of the divine connection the North Node represents and break it down into how it shows up in and what it means for your relationship.

1. There Is Something Unique and Valuable about the Connection

One of the most important aspects of the divine healthy connection is the unique value this relationship brings to your life as a whole. However, that value isn't found in financial stability, sex, social status, or having someone to keep you company so you are not alone. This connection brings your life something different from anything you've ever encountered before: it helps you with your own growth, with experiencing and building the life you desire. That is how this connection becomes one of the most valuable aspects of your life. Of course, you have to embody your own self-worth and value, but being in a relationship that adds a unique value to your life, a value that none other previously has given you, allows you to feel fully invested in the connection and also to tell yourself logically why, no matter what happens, it is worth it.

2. You Are Confident That No One Else Can Compare to Who Your Partner Is

To commit to a relationship isn't just to know the inherent value of the connection but to feel, all the way down to your bones, that you could search the world over and find no one else like the person you love. In this connection, you feel confident not just that the relationship adds value, but that this person is so unique, so interesting, intelligent, loving — whatever it may be that's important to you — that you know you will never find someone better. Once you have reached the healing adult phase of life, you are more likely to honor and admit the fact that just because there are many fish in the sea doesn't mean that any two will ever be the same. When you feel confident in your partner being the only one for you and the only one you want, then you also enter into a different type of relationship.

3. You Actively Desire to Build a Life Together

One of the biggest differences in this connection is that both people actively want to create a life together. Not only is the relationship seen as valuable and each person as unique, but you each crave spending your life together, in whatever way that means for you. While this relationship often brings more of an untraditional form of commitment, such as living apart until children are grown or retaining individual homes for the sake of having personal space, you will still actively strive to cocreate and show up for each other in all the ways that you can. Actively desiring to build a life together means each person is clear with their intentions and their desires; it means each person is progressing the relationship by meeting friends and family, planning trips, and talking about the future together. Regardless of how long you've been in relationship or what unknowns might exist, there is the feeling that you are on the path of life together, and because of that you are committed to building a shared life full of as much love and joy as possible.

4. You Are Willing to Do Whatever It Takes

While actively desiring to build a life together is one step, it can't happen without the passion and drive to do it no matter what it takes.

This is the purpose of action. It's not enough to simply dream with a partner. To commit to following through on your shared dream regardless of what obstacles arise is often the most challenging aspect. A love like this is amazing, it is incredible, and it only comes around once in a lifetime, but it also will often ask you to put it all on the line to make it work. You may have to walk away from a previous unhealthy relationship, to let go of caring what others think, to find a sense of compromise within the connection, or to learn what it means to prioritize your connection as deeply as you have your own healing and growth. This great love will take you out of your comfort zone; it will ask that you communicate as adults; it will inspire you to go to great heights for it. Through all of that, its success comes down to being willing to do whatever it takes. While you may have felt this in your karmic union, it is not the same thing this time round. This connection won't be about overlooking unhealthy traits or patterns, nor will it ask you to sacrifice your self-worth or authenticity. Instead, it will rise up to meet you where you are.

5. You Are Challenged to Grow, Do Better, and Become Your Best Self

This is the most interesting aspect of your divine healthy love connection: not only does it meet you where you are, it also inspires you to keep growing. Just because you've had to go through all your karmic lessons to reach this point doesn't mean the journey is over. In fact, learning to receive, to communicate in a healthy way, to practice boundaries with someone you love can be among the most challenging lessons you'll face. Your unhealthy love was actually in a way easier, because you didn't have to grow in order to sustain it. In this one, you will.

You and your partner will challenge each other in healthy ways to reflect on coping skills, life choices, communication styles, and personal habits; unconsciously, you are continually seeking to help each other become your best selves. To become your best self — or ever-evolving better self — is to be willing to show up with an open heart and a willingness to learn. There is no becoming better if we can't take accountability for the choices of our past and also no way to learn if we don't. This is a union that challenges the way you've previously lived to help you continue to grow. It's as if once those inner child wounds are healed, your adult self has to actually learn how to show up in a healthy relationship, and that takes time. But as this new type of relationship progresses, it honors growth and healing, which also becomes one of the strongest aspects of your foundation together. As long as you are growing together, you will never grow apart.

This is the power and draw of the North Node. It's also what generates that magic and destiny that you feel within this connection. It may take time to become accustomed to, as it's unlike the karmic toxicity that previously made you feel desperate and crazy, but it arrives to show you that real love — the magic of which two hearts are capable — lies within the peace and ease created in a healthy relationship.

While love isn't logical, it doesn't mean that you shouldn't be able to say why your partner is of value or what they bring to your life. In the 2008 romcom *Made of Honor*, Hannah travels to Scotland and falls in love with an incredible man, Colin; a whirlwind fairy-tale relationship ensues. Yet as she's sitting with the pastor preparing the wedding ceremony alongside her best friend, Tom, the pastor asks her why she fell in love with Colin, what it is about him that she is so enamored by. Hannah just smiles and shrugs, left speechless. This is the opposite of what happens with the divine healthy love. In this connection, not only will you be able to speak clearly about your amazing connection, but you will be able to describe exactly what traits you admire in your partner and what they add to your life in ways that no one else can.

But we all have to go through the process of discovering what love isn't before we can learn what it is. One of the best pieces of advice I ever received was from my Babcia, the Polish word for "grandmother." She had recently been admitted to the hospital, and I was going over every day to see her. This day, I brought pink nail polish, the color I used to paint seashells with her when I was still her little Kasha. As I sat on the end of her bed and painted her nails, we spoke in the late afternoon sun, our love warming the room. I was divorcing at the time, and when I began to tell her about it, she replied that she already knew, looking off into the distance. At this point, we already suspected that she had Alzheimer's. However, I enjoyed embracing the moments of complete clarity and intuitive knowing she still had. Then she sat up and took my hand in hers and said, "Kasha, the next time you fall in love, make sure to take your head with you." I laughed, but she patted my hand as she always did and said, "I mean it."

She always knew more than she let on, but in this case, she was especially right. No matter how illogical love might feel, we all have to be able to take our heads with us. Don't let this feel like it steals the magic from you; really, it only confirms that it's safe to trust, to believe, and to wish on shooting stars together.

The North Node across the Zodiac

To begin to understand how to read the North Node in your astrology chart and that of your partner, it is important to remember this node governs your fate, which arrives only after you have learned your karmic lessons. The first thing to notice when looking at the North Node placements is if your North Node sign is reflected in your partner's North Node, sun, or significant other placements, as this will be the case in the divine healthy love. Once you've done that, the next thing to consider is what does that mean when it comes to your fate, your relationship future, and any other lessons that might become important because of the placements.

Sometimes you will share not only the same North Node as your partner but also the same South Node. This isn't negative so long as you've both already gone through your karmic relationships; if you have, it only creates a deeper basis of understanding. It means that you've actually been moving through parallel journeys in life and have had to learn similar lessons. Now that you have, you are ready to step into your fate.

Other than sharing the same North Node, in the divine healthy love connection we often see a crossover between one person's North Node and the other's sun sign. For example, if your North Node is in Sagittarius, then your partner's North Node or sun may be in Sagittarius. On very rare occasions, it may show up as multiple placements within the chart, such as your partner having Venus, Mercury, and/or the moon in Sagittarius. The idea here is that wherever your North Node is should be reflected in your partner's chart in some significant way. This shows that you have a clear path forward. While specific matches are more usually identified with twin flame dynamics, you can still find an energy complementary to your North Node that will allow you to keep growing together.

In working with the North Node, it's important to focus on what it means for you to step personally into your own fate before looking at how it defines a relationship that will manifest in your life. The fate represented by the North Node is yours, and your healthy divine love relationship will be a significant part of that divine destiny and never contradict it. When you're reflecting on incorporating your North Node into your life, you also must remember that the goal isn't to choose your North Node over your South Node or to abandon any part of you, but instead to find a healthy balance that works for you. To truly step into your North Node means you have healed your South Node as well and can now merge together the best parts of yourself.

A client named Diedra had chosen herself over her karmic union, had walked away from it, and was just beginning to heal when John came into her life. This wasn't a connection she had planned for, but she was open to love even if she was still healing, and so she gave it a chance. After they'd been dating for a few months, she was ready to receive the truth about the connection, and so she asked me to do a reading of their charts.

The first thing that I noticed was that they shared the North Node in Pisces, as well as having complementary Venus signs. At first glance, this absolutely looked to be the healthy divine love that she was seeking, especially as she had finally ended her ten-year karmic relationship. But to better tell if it was a divine healthy connection for both of them, I asked her about his relationship history. He had never married but had had significant relationships, which had caused great heartbreak and brought him closer to his own healing and growth.

DIEDRA	
Sun	Aries
Moon	Libra
Mercury	Libra
Venus	Capricorn
Mars	Aries
Jupiter	Sagittarius
Saturn	Gemini
Uranus	Libra
Neptune	Sagittarius
Pluto	Virgo
North Node	Pisces
South Node	Virgo
Rising	Pisces

JOHN	
Sun	Pisces
Moon	Capricorn
Mercury	Aquarius
Venus	Taurus
Mars	Sagittarius
Jupiter	Sagittarius
Saturn	Taurus
Uranus	Libra
Neptune	Sagittarius
Pluto	Virgo
North Node	Pisces
South Node	Virgo
Rising	Cancer

As she described her relationship with John in more detail — the way he was continually present for the relationship, sought out meeting her friends and family, and was becoming important to her life — it felt more and more like this was the relationship she'd always desired. She mentioned that they'd begun to spend every weekend together and were already talking about marriage. This was not surprising. By the time we do reach this relationship, we know ourselves deeply, and the connection tends to progress more quickly because when it's right, you know. When it's not, it takes more time and energy to recognize that it's not (as you try to convince yourself that it is).

Diedra breathed a sigh of relief as we spoke. She had thought this was different — she knew he wasn't her karmic connection — but she wanted to make sure. And this is what I love about being able to see our fate written in the stars: not because it's a cheat sheet for relationships, but because it can be used to validate our own thoughts and experiences.

So make your own choices, let your heart lead you, but use your North Node to confirm to yourself that you really have grown as much as you feel. Let it validate your choices and open up your heart more deeply, because when a love comes around only once in a lifetime, it deserves for you to put your all in. Many times we can only do that when we are sure we have broken the cycle, when we are positive that we aren't repeating the past, and when we can see we are only beginning to write the beautiful new future we've been dreaming of.

The Meaning of Your North Node

The North Node in Aries

Your Fate Affirmation: *I trust myself to make decisions and be the creator of my own life.*

With your North Node in Aries, you have to move to a place of leadership and confidence in your life. While the lessons of the South Node in Libra have prepared you for this moment, ultimately it is your choice to step into this place or not. You are an individual and deserve to believe in yourself and in your dreams so that you can commit to living a life that is divinely meant for you.

As a North Node in Aries, you have the keen ability to take charge of life and let your passions lead you, so ensuring that your partner has a similar drive will matter significantly. You desire to live life on your terms, and while you have struggled with prioritizing your needs in the past, when you step into the fate of your North Node, you now are in the place to seize all that is meant for you. The more that you honor your inner truth, your ability to focus on what you want to create, and the more you are able to listen to and trust yourself, the further you will go. You will have a strong desire to create something of meaning with your partner, which is an important factor in your feeling connected to them.

Inevitably, you are destined for success, but you are also meant to define a new precedent in life. As you step more deeply into this fate, you are embracing your ability to focus on what you desire and manifest unlike any other — but remember to balance that with the lessons you learned in your Libra South Node. Especially in love, it's not about one partner being right and the other wrong, but about both being on the same page to figure out what is right together.

The North Node in Taurus

Your Fate Affirmation: *I deserve a life that nourishes me and provides comfort and love.*

The North Node in Taurus allows you to find a balance between the stability you seek in life and the passion and intensity of the South Node in Scorpio. For you, realizing that you don't have to choose between something that is exciting and something that is healthy is what sets you free to be able to create whatever you wish for your life.

As a Taurus North Node, you have a desire for a comfortable life surrounded by abundance and beauty. After you leave behind the lack mentality that is often associated with the South Node in Scorpio, you are able to fully embrace your inner sense of worthiness. It's this inner worthiness that will inevitably create the stability that you seek in life. When you learn this, everything in life changes.

Instead of hanging onto relationships or situations because you fear change, you will know that regardless of what happens, you will be okay because you have created within yourself what you've been seeking in life. In a relationship, as a developed North Node in Taurus, you need for your partner to have a similar idea of what life together will look like and not have your desires seen as frivolous. By wanting a certain type of home, lifestyle, or relationship, you're not being superficial — instead it means you know clearly what you desire from life.

As you honor your aspirations for your life and prioritize what matters to you, which is setting up a life that comforts your soul, you will also be able to attract the relationship that honors that. When you release the idea that in order to have passion, you have to sacrifice stability, you are able to create a new paradigm of love for yourself, one where you can continually grow with your partner, experience life together, and feel like you are surrounded by the best of everything.

The North Node in Gemini

Your Fate Affirmation: *I am able to embrace every facet of who I am as I honor both my strengths and my weaknesses.*

With your North Node in a sign that represents duality, you are tasked with finding balance between the wants of your human and the needs of your soul. You will know when you are embracing your North Node in Gemini because it no longer feels like you are at war with yourself. Self-acceptance is a huge step for you. When you honor both parts of yourself and the full spectrum of your desires, you will be able to create a life and a relationship that honor that.

As a North Node in Gemini, you can find it challenging to move past the lessons of the South Node in Sagittarius, in which you are encouraged to focus on what's in front of you instead of always thinking that something better is out there. The key to mastering this lesson is to honor your own inner truth. No matter the relationship, you can't know if it aligns with you or not if you are not being yourself. And so, as you step into the fate of your North Node, you are gaining the knowledge of what it means to embrace every facet of yourself.

When you've moved through the necessary healing, it means you accept yourself fully and have learned how the human and the soul can work together. It means that instead of your human wanting not to be alone, your soul has learned that you also don't want to be with just anyone for the sake of company, and so these two parts of you find a common ground within to live from. Once you reach the healing adult phase of life, these two sides will have found peace together, which will open up in you a huge well of empathy and understanding for others.

As you further engage your North Node in Gemini, it's important to focus on how you can continually learn and grow without thinking that the answer is in another relationship. Lean into the important qualities of the healthy divine love and open yourself to explore higher learning, adventures, and travel with your partner. Let yourself change the interior of your home around with the seasons, but don't let that movement of air energy take you away from the best relationship of your life simply because you had a desire to shake things up.

The North Node in Cancer

Your Fate Affirmation: *I am creating a life based on stability, authenticity, and love.*

As an individual with your North Node in Cancer, the home and family you establish become your top priority, but only because you've learned the lessons of the South Node in Capricorn. The North Node in Cancer is about being able to blend multiple parts of your life to create a sense of stability and authenticity. As you follow your own dreams, honor your truth, and set up a life and career that nurture your soul, then you will also be better able to cherish those you love.

The North Node in Cancer often has to learn that stereotypical success isn't the biggest determinant of a happy and fulfilling life. But to learn that requires change: it means you must practice honoring your emotional feelings as much as your logical choices. If you find that you do need to make a change in your life, it's a sign that you should allow yourself to prioritize your emotions over any sense of stability you have in your life. With the South Node in Capricorn, you have a tendency to look at how much time you've put into that unfulfilling career or relationship and then talk yourself out of trying something new, but by embracing the North Node in Cancer, you prioritize your emotional well-being and success over how your life may appear to others.

As you honor your own feelings, you start to see that it's your relationships with others that will be the determining factor in your life. Even if you have the most amazing career, if you don't feel settled into a home or have a stable and consistent relationship, then you will tend to feel like something is lacking. Use this knowledge to ensure that you are building the full life that you desire. The more stable and loving you make your home, the more grounded and productive you become in life.

Embrace your ability to feel and to create a joyful and loving home, but never forget that you don't have to give up what is most important to you in order to do those things. Be yourself, have your dreams, and let yourself also have the home, family, and relationship that you desire. Because you're here to prove you can have it all.

The North Node in Leo

Your Fate Affirmation: *I am honoring how I feel about my life as I commit to following my heart.*

The North Node in Leo asks you to release the idea that you have to protect yourself from the very things in life that you most want. The South Node in Aquarius can keep you emotionally detached from relationships or other aspects of life, as you fear having your heart broken, but to fully create what you seek, you have to trust the direction your heart is guiding you toward.

The South Node in Aquarius was all about learning that your life doesn't have to look like anyone else's; ultimately, it's more important how it feels to you. A life that looks good to others but feels to you like it's lacking is never going to bring you all you desire. The more that you can release your picture of how you thought life should go, the more you can let go of needing to make others think you're already living the perfect life, the happier you will be.

The North Node in Leo reminds you that your greatest asset is your heart and that to follow that is to find your bliss. Honor your feelings above everything else and let yourself create whatever resonates the most deeply with your soul. There is no rule book for life, so there's nothing you should ever feel like you have to live up to. When you realize that your heart is your compass for life, you will find that you have a clear direction forward.

The more you honor your heart and embrace your desire to live life fully, the happier and more grounded you will feel. Use your passion to create all you desire and then choose a partner who feels the same, so you can set the world on fire together. In relationships, you have to feel a great deal of passion with your partner, not just for each other but for life. Never forget why you grew in love in the first place, and let yourself experience life to the highest degree together so that you can both feel fueled by your relationship.

The North Node in Virgo

Your Fate Affirmation: *I embrace gratitude for all I have created in my life, even if it differs from how I imagined it would be.*

Those who have their North Node in Virgo have had to learn what unconditional love is at the hands of the South Node in Pisces and also need to have the necessary boundaries in place to protect it. As someone who has stepped into the fate of their North Node in Virgo, you are grounded and dedicated to creating the life you know you deserve, and you've released any codependency or perfectionist traits that have kept happiness at bay.

With the South Node in Pisces, you have had to understand the greater meaning of events in your life, as well as your own sense of spirituality, which has enabled you to broaden your perspective. When it comes to learning your lessons and stepping into your fate, you can have that sense of unconditional love, but also recognize that it doesn't determine how something will actually look once it has manifested. By releasing the checkbox system for life, you open up space so the universe can surprise you.

The best relationship isn't the one that you plan for, but the one that comes along and ruins your carefully planned checklist. Let yourself go all in on a love that makes you feel connected to yourself and the world around you. As a North Node in Virgo, you have an enormous healing capability, and making a contribution with your partner along these lines — like giving back to your community by doing volunteer work together — would satisfy that desire in a healthy way.

You have a great capacity to envision the future and focus on what you need to do in order to accomplish your goals, but make sure you slow down and focus on the present moment, too. This will allow you to find gratitude for all you've created and all you have in your life. By honoring the unconditional love you have for yourself, practicing healthy boundaries, and learning to create space for the divine workings of the universe, you can build a life and a relationship that are far better than you could ever have imagined.

The North Node in Libra

Your Fate Affirmation: *I am creating a life that honors all of who I am, as I know I deserve to be treated with care and respect.*

With your North Node in Libra, you will learn that working on everything together is better than struggling to do things by yourself. Many times in relationships, you feel you must choose between being right or being in love. Yet it's the lessons of the South Node in Aries and the fate of the North Node in Libra that end up teaching you there never had to be a choice. Let yourself find a balance in all things, but most importantly in how you care for yourself and what dynamics you allow in your relationship.

As you step into the fate of your North Node in Libra, you've learned that your way doesn't necessarily mean it's the best or only way to do something. You've also moved past the hyperindependence that is often a trauma response from having to do everything on your own, so you are growing more trusting of others and allowing them to be there for you in the ways that you need them to.

There is no perfection; there is only the willingness to try your best each day. As a person with the North Node in Libra, being able to work together, find compromise, and create a true partnership will be incredibly important in your relationship. This kind of dynamic also brings healing to those Aries wounds caused by feeling like you need to do everything on your own. As you open yourself up to a partnership, remember that you don't need to sacrifice your inner peace in order to make a relationship last. You also need to make sure that you're not allowing any self-sabotaging old wounds to come into play. Focus on working together, being open to learning, and continually holding space for you and your partner to share and talk matters through. This is how you can create the healthiest relationship possible.

Libra is one of the ruling signs of Venus, and building a loving partnership is one of the things that you do best. Because of this you tend to gravitate toward great commitment. Let yourself open your heart, advocate for what you need, and remind yourself that you aren't alone in this relationship. As you do, you will come to experience the joy in being able to grow with another for a lifetime.

The North Node in Scorpio

Your Fate Affirmation: *I embrace a passionate and stable life and allow the truth to lead me forward.*

As you step into the fate of your North Node in Scorpio, you allow yourself to honor the truth of your soul more deeply than ever before. You understand that your desires are based on your need for a powerful and intense relationship. Instead of succumbing to the challenges of the South Node in Taurus, you learn to trust yourself enough to pursue what you truly want from life and love.

As a person with your North Node in Scorpio, you have a deep capacity for understanding others and a very passionate nature. You may have attempted to suppress these qualities while you were in your lesson phase, as you likely tried everything possible to prioritize what seemed safe and comfortable, even if you were deeply unsatisfied with life. But as you've progressed, you've learned to honor your own truth, and you've realized that you can create what you genuinely need from life as long as you allow yourself to step into your inner power.

To move away from the South Node in Taurus means that you're not going to keep a relationship together for the sake of others or because you're resisting change; instead, you are allowing yourself to transform in all the ways necessary to create the life you dream of. In

Scorpio the North Node directs you to transform your darkness into light, meaning that the biggest challenges that you got through will also often lead to your biggest blessings. But to undergo that transformation, you have to trust yourself.

In this process you can learn to dance with logic: you don't talk yourself out of your best ideas, but neither do you forgo growth because of a momentary feeling. When you can tap into your inner darkness, honor your truth, and surrender to your innate intensity for life, you are able to create the magical, passionate relationship you've always felt calling to your soul. Life truly can be balanced; your lesson is learning never to compromise the truth of your soul because you fear change. Through your North Node transformation, the most beautiful moments await.

The North Node in Sagittarius

Your Fate Affirmation: *I am free to be myself and create the life that resonates with my heart.*

The North Node in Sagittarius asks you to embrace your higher self and to focus on the lessons that you've moved through in life. Oftentimes, with the South Node in Gemini, you can feel boxed into being one particular way or as if life offers so many options, it's hard to trust which one is meant for you. But on this journey into your fate, you are guided to concentrate on yourself and get to know who you authentically are, because that is the key to the love relationship you've always longed for.

The South Node in Gemini can make you somewhat wishy-washy as you adjust yourself for the comfort of others or retain a fear of going deeply into the greater meaning of events. However, by embracing your North Node in Sagittarius, you are able to become both the student and the teacher. You honor your soul by allowing yourself to follow the direction of your higher self, and you never settle for the mediocre when you know you are meant for greatness.

As you step into the fate held in your North Node in Sagittarius, you come to a deep acceptance of yourself. You are no longer waiting for someone else to set you free, because you have done that for yourself. Focusing on your priorities and goals becomes incredibly important, especially since you will always carry that duality energy of Gemini within you. When you know your truth and honor the higher purpose of events in your life, then you can be confident in whatever direction your heart is leading you.

In relationships, your most important need will be for your connection to feel like it supports your path of growth. You may desire to have a shared purpose or understanding with your partner, but ultimately you will have to feel like your relationship sustains your continued journey of developing your authentic self and experiencing all that life has to offer. When you can receive this from a partner, you have the perfect space to create a relationship that will only continue to teach you what it means to genuinely love and be loved.

The North Node in Capricorn

Your Fate Affirmation: *I am deserving of a fully abundant life that is filled with success, joy, and love.*

As you focus on embracing the fate of your North Node, you are also finding autonomy within yourself and your life. On this journey you abandon neither those you love the most nor the life you dream of living; rather, you come to understand how you can actually have both. Whatever you believe is possible is ultimately what you end up creating.

With the South Node in Cancer, you often need to move through the lesson of no longer sacrificing yourself for others or thinking that your relationship defines your success in life. But as you do, you also start to ground your emotions and make your decisions from a more stable place. The power for you rests in understanding that no one's happiness is more important than yours, no matter who they are or how much you might love them. The North Node in Capricorn asks you to focus on your own path ahead and find a balance between being there for others and never neglecting yourself again.

Oftentimes, finding your individual career or purpose becomes essential to the North Node in Capricorn, so having a partner who will continually support and encourage you to pursue your dreams will be important. But so is ensuring that you both have a healthy sense of self. You will need to be in a relationship of true equals; otherwise, you'll feel like you must give up on your dreams or desires in order to show up in the way your partner is asking — especially if what they want from you is unhealthy in any way.

Someone with a healthy North Node in Capricorn has a meaningful and enriching romantic life, along with a focused and directed life of their own, which includes a successful career. As you honor yourself, you also create the space for your partner not only to find their own life direction — ultimately, this is what fosters a connection that respects your independence — but also to always be there for you with a kind word, soft touch, and open heart.

The North Node in Aquarius

Your Fate Affirmation: *I allow myself to create the life that fits my unique needs and to embrace the support of those I care about.*

Freedom is the most important thing to you if you have your North Node in Aquarius — not necessarily the freedom to be able to do whatever you want, but the freedom to create a life and listen to the unique call of your soul. The more that you can move away from the idea that life has to look a certain way or that there is one specific way to create a relationship, the happier and more fulfilled you will be.

The South Node in Leo has taught you the lessons that appearance isn't everything and that while listening to your heart is crucial, that should be balanced with honoring the needs of those you care about the most. The North Node in Aquarius gives you a decisively different way of viewing life, and because of that, you tend to approach situations as the epitome of the free spirit. You crave adventure, individuality, and being able to create something that the world has never seen before — but you also need to ensure you're creating in deep connection with your heart and not just for the sake of being different.

When you honor your uniqueness, then you can see that it's not something that needs to be proven, but only lived. The tendency of the South Node in Leo to focus on how things look will dissipate the more that you validate yourself, one of the most important lessons for you. When you can self-validate, then you are no longer seeking the attention or approval of others from an unhealthy state, nor are you just trying to assert your independence. This creates the space of ultimate freedom, because now you are not trying to prove anything to others or to yourself.

When it comes to love, you need to be able to let yourself create whatever feels like it will suit your life, which means that attracting a similar free spirit is crucial. As you incorporate compromise into your relationship and let yourself own the power of being who you authentically are, you also strengthen your capacity to tap into your deep well of emotional empathy, which then leads to a stronger connection with your partner. And as you progress on your journey, validating yourself and dismantling those walls around your heart, you'll come to see the only right way to love is the one that aligns with your own truth.

The North Node in Pisces

Your Fate Affirmation: *I am able to practice healthy boundaries as I open my heart to explore the greater meaning of life and my connections with others.*

The North Node in Pisces asks you to embrace your relationship with the spiritual realm, to open to the deeper meaning of life, and to surrender to the process of discovering what it means to be a human. As you do this — progressing away from the fear and perfectionist energy of the South Node in Virgo — you will find the compassion and grace for yourself that allow you to feel like you're truly becoming your best version of you.

When you begin your journey with the South Node in Virgo, you often have to learn that releasing fixed ideas of how things will go is incredibly important to achieving the success and love you desire in life. Virgo is very analytical and can get stuck trying to figure everything out, but in certain situations, the answer that the logical mind is searching for isn't one you're really needing to discover, and that is what leads you into a deeper relationship with spirit. By embracing your own divinity and your connection to the universe, you can develop an appreciation for the ebbs and flows of life while retaining faith that everything that's meant for you is possible.

Those with the North Node in Pisces are the ultimate romantics, and so love here has to take on the allure of quality time, dates, flowers, and poetry — along with stability. You crave that true, once-in-a-lifetime soul connection, but to be able to embrace it, you have to allow life to move differently than how you imagined it would. The duality of the North Node in Pisces is the conscious and unconscious mind, and the South Node in Virgo is the healing earth sign. The lesson here is that you can heal yourself; you can bring together any division and find the best of romance *and* consistency.

In relationships, trust becomes incredibly important; you need to feel that in order to truly surrender to your South Node lessons. You need to learn how to trust yourself as well — often an important lesson you are guided to learn before entering into a healthy divine relationship. Because both Pisces and Virgo are known to have a tendency toward self-sacrifice and codependency, it's important to make sure you are honoring your feelings and needs in a relationship, so that you can feel that delicious balance of reciprocity. As you allow yourself to heal, to practice setting boundaries, and to release the idea that there is a perfect way to love, you are able to see that the divine has been guiding you all along and that the reward is always worth the wait.

The Astrology of Healing within a Divine Love

The ultimate expression of love is to be found in the healing qualities that it provides. In your soulmate and karmic relationships, triggers arose that were meant to help you become aware of your own wounds that needed healing. These triggers were painful, explosive at times, and revealing as they sought to expose the very parts of yourself that you needed to see. But in a divine love, a different type of healing is available. In this connection, you will still be triggered, but it happens through presence, through love, and through being challenged to receive all you have ever desired.

So many times, when I speak with clients across this beautiful world, they express a misunderstanding about why this amazing, healthy relationship can still feel so challenging at times. As they do, I smile and sigh, because it's only in a truly healthy, cycle-breaking relationship that being triggered *to receive* occurs. When you are operating from your child or teenager, unconsciously seeking what you never received or that which replicates what you did receive, relationships feel a lot easier. In truth, those relationships that mirror the dynamic of karmic lessons, at least in the beginning, will always be easier to receive, simply because that dynamic is already familiar to the wounds of the inner child or teen.

The purpose of healing and growth isn't just to improve yourself but also to change your relationships for the better. This is where divine love differs from the soulmate and karmic connections: it will trigger you, and it will ask you to face your walls, your fears, your coping mechanisms — but it's going to do it through love and through presence. It's as if the previous relationships helped you heal those wounds that you thought equated to love, and now that you know they don't — at least not the kind of forever love you've been searching for — it's up to you to learn how to receive the love you have always craved.

In fact, the healing of the divine love connection comes down mostly to learning to receive. Many times, at first, this love feels too easy to accept. The connection can be challenging initially as you suddenly realize you don't need to fight to be seen, to have your needs met, or to feel understood, because an organic ease is present in this relationship. And that is why you have to go through multiple lessons to learn to accept it. Moreover, you also need to explore your own conditioning that has you pushing away a love that genuinely only wants to love.

To be triggered into healing is the purpose of divine love. But because of this triggering, I often receive the question "How do you know if it's a karmic union or divine love?" First, usually only those in karmic relationships ask that, because they are trying to justify or console their inner child into accepting something that they already know isn't healthy. Second, know that you will be triggered in every relationship you are in, and if you aren't, then that means there is no growth or healing potential present within the connection. But while the karmic relationship triggers through pain, betrayal, toxicity, and wounding, the divine love relationship triggers through receiving, understanding, presence, and crystal-clear intention. No matter what it goes through, the karmic relationship never turns out any different, whereas the divine love connection is always evolving — not only do both people become better, but so does the union that they build.

Ultimately, to receive the divine love connection into your life and heart, you would had to have healed your inner child to the degree that this part of you no longer self-sabotages or pushes away what it's always desired, because it is no longer afraid of receiving the goodness. As we've discussed before, the purpose of the karmic relationship is ultimately to teach you that only you can give your inner child what it's always needed, through the process of reparenting that inner self. The divine love union, on the other hand, helps open you up so that each part of you can be showered with the love you've always desired and needed.

Your Inner Child Was Always Worthy

You were always worthy of the love you desired. Your inner child was worthy of being nurtured and cared for, and your inner teenager was worthy in your radical authenticity. You were and are worthy simply because you were born being so. Yet most childhoods make you question that fact. Know that this is for the sole purpose of having you learn how to love yourself, learn what that means and looks like. And, as everything in life is connected, your divine love relationship will carry important trademarks of your childhood. Rather than pointing to the wounds, however, it will point the way to the love you've had in your life.

When we dissect the wounds of our inner child, we usually find the majority of them occurred at the hands of one parent more than the other. However, in cases where both parents have contributed to feelings of abandonment and unworthiness, there is often a caregiver, aunt, family friend, or even friend of your own who has always loved you. When you are in your wounded child state, it can be hard to see the good that did surround you. But as you heal, you can start to broaden your perspective to honor the truth of who was present for you and in what ways they tried to show their love and care for you.

The healing of the divine love relationship is found within this aspect of the birth charts. This is why it's so important to go beyond your and your partner's charts and to open up your inquiry to the charts of parents and caregivers, as I call them. Just because some people who surround you do not share your blood doesn't mean that they aren't members of your soul family. When you understand that everyone is placed in your life for a purpose, then you can also see how it's not just the trauma you will repeat, but the healthy love you were shown, too.

A few years back I received a call from a woman named Kylie, who was trying to figure out the meaning of her relationships and to understand a particular connection that she had throughout her life. As we talked, we were able to identify the soulmate wound of her first marriage and the karmic healing of the relationship she had after her divorce. But there was this other connection present that was decidingly different from anything she'd experienced before.

When Kylie was only a teenager, still full of hope in high school, she had fallen in love. Kylie and Jack were the epitome of high school sweethearts, but as most young love does, it ended when they graduated. Yet despite the ending of their romantic relationship, they stayed in contact throughout their lives, always being there for each other, especially during the most challenging moments.

At first Kylie wasn't sure if perhaps Jack was her first love, if maybe she had two karmic relationships, or if her karmic relationship was actually her divine love. But we talked about the connection she and Jack shared and what they represented to each other. Their connection always came so easily, and no matter how they grew, they always accepted and understood each other. Even though the "I love yous" ceased when they were in high school, the feeling of a deep bond continued to exist between them. Kylie recalled how one time she and her daughter had run into Jack, and her daughter had asked her, "Why does that man look at you like he loves you?" After a deep sigh, Kylie had told her daughter that he did and likely always would.

KYLIE	
Sun	Aries
Moon	Scorpio
Mercury	Taurus
Venus	Cancer
Mars	Taurus
Jupiter	Scorpio
Saturn	Taurus
Uranus	Libra
Neptune	Sagittarius
Pluto	Virgo
North Node	Aquarius
South Node	Leo
Rising	Sagittarius

KYLIE'S MOTHER	
Sun	Libra
Moon	Aquarius
Mercury	Aquarius
Venus	Libra
Mars	Virgo
Jupiter	Libra
Saturn	Sagittarius
Uranus	Leo
Neptune	Scorpio
Pluto	Virgo
North Node	Aries
South Node	Libra
Rising	Scorpio

As our work progressed, Kylie understood that her marriage was indeed her soulmate relationship, while her karmic relationship was the one that she thought was her divine love, as many do. She saw that it was just meant to crack her open far enough to realize she didn't need anyone to choose or love her to know she was worthy to have what she always desired. And so that left Jack. That connection had all the qualities of the divine love relationship, except that they hadn't yet been able to come together as their healing adult selves to give their connection the chance it needed.

JACK	
Sun	Aries
Moon	Pisces
Mercury	Capricorn
Venus	Libra
Mars	Scorpio
Jupiter	Libra
Saturn	Scorpio
Uranus	Libra
Neptune	Sagittarius
Pluto	Virgo
North Node	Sagittarius
South Node	Gemini
Rising	Aquarius

JACK'S FATHER	
Sun	Capricorn
Moon	Scorpio
Mercury	Capricorn
Venus	Cancer
Mars	Capricorn
Jupiter	Cancer
Saturn	Cancer
Uranus	Gemini
Neptune	Libra
Pluto	Leo
North Node	Cancer
South Node	Capricorn
Rising	Sagittarius

All of that changed as both Kylie and Jack moved beyond their karmic relationships and once again found themselves wrapped up in the connection that always seemed to call them home. In looking at their charts, I saw a positive carryover from Kylie's mother and Jack's dad, both of which represented the most positive relationships in their childhoods. As we looked at the charts, I showed her the difference between seeking the love we've never received and finally accepting the love we have always had. Along with some other important markers in their astrology, this positive crossover represented the healing love that was always present in their connection, and it explained why they always found their way back to each other, no matter how much their lives changed.

When you look at the astrology charts of the divine love relationship, it's important to remember there is a bigger story at play within your life. If the purpose of love ultimately is to heal, then when you have healed your inner child, you will experience a new validation and confirmation from this divine romantic relationship, as you are loved in all the ways each part of you has longed for. You will see crossovers of a healthier or more reliable parent or caregiver in your partner's astrology chart, but it's not because you are meant to learn a karmic lesson once again. It's because now that you have, you can finally open to receiving the love you have always desired.

Humans naturally seek what is familiar. While you once sought wounding similar to that which you received as a child, because you believed that was what love was, you now will start seeking a healing love similar to the love that was present in your childhood but that you may not have noticed or labeled as such. This healing divine love will break all the patterns and cycles of your life. As you are able to welcome this all-encompassing relationship into your heart, it will defy what you have come to expect about love and may even challenge certain beliefs you've had about relationships.

Destroying the Picture of Perfection

When my clients begin describing the kind of partner that they envision in their life, the majority of the qualities they name end up being negotiable. For instance, I had a woman say that the gentleman needed to be of a certain height and body shape. Another client preferred a certain educational degree status. While we need to be clear on what our negotiables and nonnegotiables are, especially in this healing divine love relationship, we also have to understand the difference between someone who will actually fulfill our needs and someone who will simply embody the picture we still carry around of what we think will feel perfect.

When it comes to this relationship, after all the healing that has occurred up to this point, the idea of your negotiables and nonnegotiables becomes very important. A negotiable is something that won't ultimately determine the outcome of a relationship; it can be approached in a flexible way. A nonnegotiable, on the other hand, is something that fulfills a core need of yours, something you must have in order to maintain your healthiest and most authentic self. For example, a negotiable might be a matter of height, profession, or what type of commitment you are looking for. But a nonnegotiable would be something like a healthy partner free of addictions, financially stable, or agreeable to not having children together. Only you can know what your negotiables and nonnegotiables are — and frequently, they may be different from what you had originally thought.

The simple attributes of how you lead your life — your daily routines, or how you prefer to keep your home — might be more nonnegotiable than you have previously realized. While many people may think it's affairs that commonly end relationships, it's most often the little daily aspects of life, such as the dishes being left in the sink, or the lack of quality or alone time — the differences that become apparent only when two imperfect humans merge their lives together.

While not overtly romantic, this is part of the work in the divine love relationship: to heal that love wound from your karmic connection, you are now bringing a sense of logic to love, as I've mentioned. It's not just about incredible sex or about the relationship making sense, but about clearly discussing your negotiables and nonnegotiables in as honest and up-front a manner as you each can; this is how you build a relationship that honors the uniqueness of both partners. To heal is to ask all the questions that we often think of as unromantic — because the healing adult self understands that by doing so, you expand the space for love and magic to bloom.

Passion and the desire to connect intimately with your partner, which is an incredible part of the divine love relationship, aren't things that come out only in the darkness of the bedroom, clothed with lingerie and lace. The desire to connect physically with someone arises because of how you connect and interact with each other throughout the day. As I joke with my clients, the relationship is the cupcake, and the sex is the frosting with the cherry on top. This healthy love has a stable and nourishing base, and while the sex is amazing, it's the product of the connection itself.

I have created a list of questions to help clients identify their negotiables and nonnegotiables as they move on from their karmic cycle. Prior to this point, such a list was irrelevant, because even if you wanted to be more logical about love, your inner child was incapable of being anything other than purely emotional. As you step into your healing adult self, it's important to become aware of what it is that you genuinely need from love. This list is meant to be gone through first by you, alone, so that you can discover without reservation what resonates as your truth. Afterward and when you're ready, it can serve as an activity to do with your partner; after you've both reflected on the answers, you might compare your lists and talk about topics that arise. The idea is to embrace what actually goes into a healthy relationship while also being aware of what your negotiables and nonnegotiables are. While in your karmic relationship you may have agreed to sacrifice it all to stay in the connection, in this phase of your life, you're okay with walking away from the table if what is being served isn't what you want or what will satisfy you.

Questions to Identify Your Relationship Negotiables and Nonnegotiables

What kind of quality time with your partner do you need? Family time? Group socializing? Alone time for yourself?

How do you best communicate? What is the most effective way for others to communicate with you?

Do you need to make plans in the relationship? Short-term? Long-term?

How best do you feel supported by your partner?

How do you express your love? How do you want to receive it? What makes you feel loved and secure?

Do you need intimate physical touch (such as cuddling or hand holding) in equal measure with sexual touch (foreplay and sex), or is one more important than the other?

To feel your best, do you need to feel that you are listened to, seen, valued, given space, or supported? How do others show you that?

What type of living arrangement or sharing of space feels like it would fulfill or be in alignment with your needs?

How do you like to function in your daily routines and in the setup of your home? What are you preferences around cleaning and laundry? Are you an early riser or a night owl? Do you lean toward stereotypical household roles or partnership?

What are your spiritual needs or desire to share growth or the meaning of life with a partner? For example, are meditation, yoga, or religious services or traditions important in your life, and do you want your partner to share in them? Or do you want to pursue them independently?

How do you envision separate and shared financial resources for a home or life together, as well as ensure that both you and your partner are abundant?

What are your needs or desires for having children and building a family together? Are these nonnegotiables for you?

What are your needs in terms of commitment? Do you need or want to get married? Have a commitment ceremony? Exchange rings privately? Consciously choose each other every day?

In the healthy divine love relationship, the idea is not to choose someone others think is good for you or someone with whom you play out wounds you're unaware of, but to consciously own your truth and to choose a partner who is living in theirs. This is what creates the feeling of magic in this connection. You'll feel like you've known each other forever, because your pieces fit together in a way that you've never experienced before and never will again. Love isn't magical because it's addicting, nor because of the push and pull between the avoidant and the anxious. It's not even the impossibility of the connection that fuels desire, but rather the simple realization of, "Oh, there you are," which occurs when you are able to fully receive what you have always desired, because you've learned how to give it to yourself first. In this connection there is no lack, no fairy tale, no rescuing. It's about the coming together of two healing adults who are aware of their imperfections and yet also know they are worthy of being loved.

Clean Slate

As you progress through your journey of growth and open profoundly to a romantic connection, you will inevitably come to see love as being different from how you had previously defined it. I often say that we can't know what love is until we first learn what it isn't. It's also why the love you give yourself (or don't) sets the precedent for every other relationship you will have.

In my work with clients, we always seem to arrive at a place where they question if they've ever really loved anyone prior to their divine love relationship, because it feels so different. Of course, the love that

Understanding the Soul Truth
of Your Rising Sign

Traditionally, your rising sign — also called your ascending or ascendant sign — is the zodiac sign that was quite literally rising on the eastern horizon at the time of your birth. That sign changes every two hours or so, making it a rare and important distinction in your chart and therefore your relationships. Your rising sign is mostly known for representing your physical body and how you appear to others, but in the lens of astrology we're using, it actually symbolizes so much more.

Beyond the traditional aspects of astrology, your rising sign is a guiding force in your life, and its effects will be felt in each and every placement that you have within your chart. This is the reason why sometimes certain individuals feel they have to choose and identify more with their rising sign than their sun sign. But from my perspective, it's more helpful to see your rising sign as the umbrella under which all of your other planetary aspects lie. This means, for example, that if you are a Cancer rising and have an Aries sun and Venus in Capricorn, everything that you experience and seek will be under the umbrella of that Cancer rising energy. Your rising sign represents how you use all of the other astrology placements in your chart, which is also why it becomes so important to the divine love relationship. It doesn't matter what your sun sign is, because everything you do and want to create will be coming from the energy of your rising sign.

When you think of your rising in this way, you can see that it's almost as if it directs the energy toward what will be most important to you. For example, an Aquarius sun might be known for being untraditional, gravitating toward unique endeavors or breaking molds as they strive for autonomy and success for themselves and others. But if they have a Libra rising, then that changes their disposition, making them more focused on working with others, creating healthy partnerships, and finding balance in their lives. It's not that the energy of the sun sign is abandoned, but it takes on a new variation based on what the rising sign is. The result is more knowledge about how to honor your inner truth.

To understand yourself better is the point in astrology — who you are not just in the present but in your childhood and in your relationships as well. Interestingly, the rising sign is just as important in the karmic union as it is in the divine love relationship. In either kind of relationship, you may be drawn to someone who has the same rising sign as you or to someone who has the opposite rising sign (which means one person's rising sign falls in the other's seventh house of relationships). The way you know whether it's your karmic relationship is that in the karmic, you repeat the patterns of your childhood.

The rising sign of a divine love will resonate with your growth and will mark a difference in who you're attracting into your life. Prior to reaching this level of healing, it's likely that your parents' rising signs were reflected in the rising signs of your partners or in significant placements within their charts, especially in the relationships where you moved through learning to give yourself what you never received. But as you heal, you stop repeating what you know and instead look for someone who aligns with who you truly are.

As I've mentioned before, when you're looking at the divine love relationship, it's important to examine the charts from your whole history of significant partners, as well as your family's charts. After two or three partners, you will often see a shift from looking to receive what you never had to trying to create what you always longed for.

This will be reflected in the charts: instead of your healthy divine love partner having the same rising sign as your parents, or their Mercury and Venus being in the same sign as their rising, you'll see a difference that fits your authentic nature and also will strengthen the bond between you.

As I reflect back on the story of Kylie and Jack, I see it was their rising sign placements that helped to provide confirmation that the relationship was genuinely different from any previous ones. Besides the nature of their connection and the positive ways that each was loved by the other, they also shared the same rising sign. This meant that everything they did would be focused on setting up a life together, one that not only felt magical but also was directed by a common understanding of what is most important.

While you may have a different rising sign from your partner's in the divine healthy union, it's more common for them to be the same or to fall into the opposing sign, such as Aquarius and Leo, Aries and Libra, or Gemini and Sagittarius. The opposing sign is the one that is directly opposite on the zodiac chart from your rising sign; because of that, as I mentioned earlier, it falls into the seventh house of relationships. While you ultimately need to be the one to determine if your relationship is healthy, by understanding the relationship between your rising sign and your partner's, you will be able to embrace more of your authentic nature while also feeling secure that you and your partner truly do have similar goals for life.

The Life Lessons of Your Rising Sign

Aries Rising

Your Life Affirmation: *I am capable of creating whatever I dream of by embracing courage and believing in myself.*

If you have Aries rising, step into your inner warrior and don't be afraid to fight for what you most want. Trust in yourself to always know the direction that you are meant to take. You will need both to embrace your innate leadership qualities and to have ample room to explore the relationship with yourself. By give yourself the space to continually honor your individuality, you will be able to make the most of your strengths rather than succumbing to frustration or anger.

For you, the most important priority in life will be to leave your mark and to know that you are in charge of your own destiny. No matter where your sun sign or other planetary placements are, you will often have a natural ability to rise above. Let yourself focus on what you genuinely desire from life and believe that you can accomplish anything you desire by refusing to accept less.

Taurus Rising

Your Life Affirmation: *I deserve a life of comfort and ease as I become my best self.*

With your rising in Taurus, you are able to create a life of physical comfort and ease while also finding the stability that you seek from life. To some it might appear that you are stubborn, but it's just that you know what you are worth and what you need. Honor this by validating the importance of having financial abundance, a comfortable home, and the support in place that allows you to feel like you are living the life you are meant to have. By understanding that this Taurus energy will filter into every facet of your astrology chart, you can allow yourself some grace while you tend to the physical aspects of life, knowing that is what you need in order to honor your true self.

The life you create is important, and for you that means having a career, home, and other physical aspects that represent comfort and success. While you always need to remember to find a balance between the physical and the emotional, by honoring and validating your need for a stable life that also offers comfort or even luxury, you will be able to find the best of both worlds.

Gemini Rising

Your Life Affirmation: *I am embracing a diverse way of experiencing life through my relationships with others.*

Let yourself be who you naturally are, Gemini rising, because that is all you need to do. You are social by nature, and your relationships matter to you. You need to have fulfilling connections in your life in order to feel like you are living to your highest capability. This means not just actively exploring your important relationships with others, but also building connections that embrace and nurture the different sides of you. The more that you affirm the importance of your relationships with others, the more you will see that by experimenting with life, you can discover what truly fulfills your needs and desires.

You are someone who naturally enjoys the best parts of life — going out, staying in, and everything in between. When you can create a life in which you allow yourself to be exactly who you are, you also find that internal balance you seek. Life is meant to be lived and fully enjoyed; having a partner beside you who believes the same is often the one piece of your puzzle you need to put in place. Once you do, you will feel like you really do have it all.

Cancer Rising

Your Life Affirmation: *I am focused on creating a home and family that nurture my spirit.*

No matter what other interests or passions you have, home and family will always be the central focus of your life. Cancer rules the home, and as a rising sign, even if you desire to travel, to be a free spirit, you will still place the highest value on the home and family you create. It doesn't have to be a stereotypical vision of home, though — it won't matter if you have a four-bedroom suburban house or a flat in your favorite part of the city. Nor will it matter if you're married or you celebrate the holidays with friends. No matter what phase of life you are in, the home you create for yourself and the family you choose will be the center of your life. To live your truth, you need to honor this.

You can still be a free spirit with a home base; you can still show up for those you care about while accomplishing all of your dreams. But you get to define what that means for you, in whatever unique or authentic way feels satisfying to that desire within. As you do, you will learn that you never have to sacrifice who you are to build what matters to you.

Leo Rising

Your Life Affirmation: *I am able to be my full, radiant self as I create a life of boldness and passion.*

If your rising is in Leo, your birthright is defined by your ability to step into your power and radiate your passions to the world. This will require that you don't hide behind anything, including your wounds — that you allow yourself to truly be seen. Whether by the world or only by your partner, letting yourself be fully seen, vulnerabilities and all, lets you own the truth of who you are. You are passionate, you are bold, and sometimes you may even make a scene, but it is all for the higher purpose of living life out loud.

As you accept yourself ever more deeply, you will see that you deserve to take up space and to follow your heart. Even if the path you choose is different from most, it's not worth any less. But you have to embrace your fierce nature for yourself and refuse to water yourself down for anyone ever again. Display your passion and let yourself attract someone who has the same zest for life, so together you can set the world on fire.

Virgo Rising

Your Life Affirmation: *I deserve to heal myself first and embrace my strengths as I surround myself with those who can support me on my path.*

You have a very specific way of looking at life if your rising sign is Virgo, and while comparing yourself to stereotypes might have told you your way was wrong in the past, let yourself see your qualities as the assets that they are. You dream big dreams, and you know precisely what will fulfill them. Just because life won't go precisely according to plan doesn't mean you should ever abandon who you are. Step up to your ability to plan and figure anything out, to create amazingness from nothing, and to find a silver lining in any cloud. While everyone is unique, don't underestimate that you have the gifts capable of creating greatness.

As you embrace all of your traits, even redefining "perfectionist" as "determined," you will find that you can create all you wish. While you benefit from being asked to step out of your comfort zone every now and then, you also are precisely as you are meant to be, and when you say yes to that, you step into your fate. The details of life that matter most are those when you can work with the divine most closely. By leaning into this talent, you can create magic in any moment.

Libra Rising

Your Life Affirmation: *I embrace my relationships with others as a vehicle for self-growth while focusing on creating a life of peace and balance.*

Honor the importance of relationships with others in your life, Libra rising. While you need to ensure that you're attending to your needs and desires, the ability to work with others and create positive relationships is an asset for any life you desire to live. As you realize that no matter what, you require a sense of balance and peace in your life, you will also come to understand the importance of reciprocal relationships. You have a requirement for how you want to be treated by those in your life; know that you're not asking for too much.

Just because others may define success a certain way doesn't mean that is what will feel like success to you. Focus on your dreams and your goals, but embrace the power that different relationships can bring to your life. Let yourself delight in them. Be an amazing lover, enjoy time with your friends and siblings, and honor your talent for bringing others together, because as you do you will also come to appreciate the unique way that you see the world.

Scorpio Rising

Your Life Affirmation: *I embrace the truth in all forms while I strive to live a life of intensity and desire, allowing myself to transform as many times as necessary.*

The more you resist, the more it will persist, and so you must surrender to your desire for passion and intensity, Scorpio rising. Not everyone will value or prioritize the truth like you do, but truth is your tool to create the life of your dreams — in this space you are able to create the strongest foundation possible. While you need to ensure you're also seeking healthy dynamics on your quest for passion and intensity, never let anyone talk you into accepting less than you desire. You want a life of meaning, you believe in a once-in-a-lifetime love, and all you must do to achieve it is accept this part of yourself.

You have an innate way of being able to make magic in even the most mundane of circumstances, and because of that, others are attracted to your energy. Focus on what brings that feeling of intensity into your life in a healthy way; this will keep you from succumbing to other, less positive temptations. Not everyone craves a passionate, intense existence, but you do; owning that allows you to accept yourself for who you really are.

Sagittarius Rising

Your Life Affirmation: *I am free to be myself and explore the amazing complexities of life while knowing that I am loved by those who mean the most to me.*

If Sagittarius is your rising, you must be the one to seek your own freedom instead of resting it in the hands of others. By embracing your spirit to explore and experience life, you allow yourself to become who you truly are. Relationships are important to you and help you create a life of substance, but you need to discover what both of those things mean for you. When you ascertain what and who resonate with your truth, you have equipped yourself to create the life you've dreamed of, the life you need on a soul level.

Recognize that you will always be searching for the greater meaning within events and relationships in your life. While you will have to know yourself before you can be certain about what resonates for you, your ability to explore life's different depths is an asset. Ultimately you can build a life that is based on your freedom to live your authentic purpose and destiny. Create what calls to you and trust your soul to always give you the confirmation that you are on the right path.

Capricorn Rising

Your Life Affirmation: *I am a vessel of success when I honor my innate abilities and overcome any challenges.*

There is nothing wrong with success, Capricorn rising. No matter whether it's your career, your love, or creating a life you can be proud of, you will be successful when you embrace your inner genius and ability to overcome whatever obstacles may cross your path. You are incredibly determined and focused; just check in with yourself from time to time to make sure that the path you are on will lead to the goal you desire. But never feel like you are wrong for wanting to make a success of everything you touch. The more you can honor your need to achieve a professional and personal life that is everything you ever have dreamed of, the gentler and more accepting toward yourself you will become.

To be on a path of success means to always try your best, to look for ways to continually improve situations and relationships in your life, and to never to give up. You are capable of going to great lengths to create what you want, but to actually find what you seek, make sure that you are giving attention to all of the important areas of your life. Remember, business success will never take the place of personal accomplishment, just as you can't feel bad if you want more from life than an amazing relationship. When you can discover what success means for you and achieve it, you will truly be able to live your dream.

Aquarius Rising

Your Life Affirmation: *I am uniquely myself and trust that the universe will always reveal my divine fate at precisely the right moment.*

The more you embrace your authentic self, the easier everything gets if you have Aquarius rising. You want to do things differently from others, because you have an unmatched, unique vision when it comes to life. Welcome the fact that you can see things in a way that others can't, but don't wait around for everyone else to be on board. You need to trust yourself and let yourself do things in whatever way most resonates with your soul; as you do, you will discover how to lead by example through your own purpose. While you enjoy being the rebel of the zodiac, you do so only because you understand how you can improve things for yourself and others. Recognize this as an asset and surround yourself with those who will support you in your mission to change the world.

You will always need a bit more time to yourself than other zodiac signs, so that you can tune into your inner self and focus on the matter at hand. It doesn't mean you should cling to hyperindependence, but by taking the time you need for yourself, you can show up for others in all the ways you desire. The more you allow yourself to be who you truly are, the more you will comprehend that you were made for a divine purpose in this life.

Pisces Rising

Your Life Affirmation: *I am connected to my heart and allow myself to feel the world around me as I strive to discover the greater meaning within life.*

You are a spiritual muse, Pisces rising: while you are in your search for the greater meaning within life, you often end up helping others discover theirs. Though others may disregard your idealistic or dreamy nature, you do have a gift to see beyond the surface of things, which means you are here to create something that is new and different. Whether it's about love or about your soul purpose, you need to allow yourself to dream and see the world as only you do. There is no need here to fit yourself into a tight, labeled box; you are meant to defy all the norms and expectations.

Let your emotions rule your life, but find your grounding as well. There is nothing wrong with living with your head in the clouds, as long as your feet are planted on the ground, at least most of the time. You inspire others simply by being yourself, because you see things as they should be. Focus on honoring your spiritual connection and continue to work toward creating a life and a relationship based on what you know can be real. You are guaranteed to create whatever you wish, for the divine is always on your side.

Your Truth Is Always Worth Living

When you fully embrace all that you are, you step into a new way of living your life. Not only will you have you reached the healing adult phase, but you will have done the deep work to incorporate the different facets of yourself into one wild, cohesive, authentic being. It can often feel like it takes a lifetime to discover and embrace who that person is, but once you do, you don't need to be anything other than who you are.

Regardless of where you are on that path, it is always worth exploring, because the moments of learning are just as valuable as reaching the destination. As a quote popularly attributed to Ralph Waldo Emerson says, "It's not the destination, but the journey that matters." I would add that it's the journey that has the greater meaning: it's what actually *creates* the destination. When you think of love, it seems that the healthy divine love becomes the destination, but even your definition of that shifts as you learn more about yourself. For many, originally this idea of a romantic destination was being married and living in a home with a few kids. But as many find out, just because you have acquired the milestones you believed represented love doesn't mean you have the relationship you truly desire. And so you leave, you learn, you grow, you have a few moments you'd never tell anyone about, and you accumulate your fair share of heartbreak. But in that process you also discover what it means to genuinely love and be loved. How it's more than just fairy tales and romance, more than just a shared mortgage and holidays where you look like the perfect family. You learn that it's found in the authentic connection between two people who have consciously decided that life is better when they show up as their true selves. This is how they grow into a love that really does last a lifetime.

Whenever I speak with clients, I always say I firmly believe the universe took me on the path it did just so that I could experience almost anything that one could go through in this life. When I say I have been there, I really have. When I say that I never suggest anything I wouldn't do myself, I genuinely mean it, because, like everyone else, I had to go through my darkest moments to be able to discover who I truly am. I began this journey as my soulmate marriage was crumbling around me; I had realized that, after being together for over a decade, I had no idea who I was anymore or really if I ever even did. I had forgotten all about that girl in high school who had a way with words and believed in experiencing life with an open heart.

Thankfully for me, I have always had an amazing connection who returned at that time with a letter I'd given him when I was only sixteen. As he slid it across the table to me, he said he hoped to remind me of who I really am. And eventually I was able to repay him with the same. But even with his support, it's still been a journey to discover my truth and to realize that the only life worth living is one that is based on that truth. It doesn't matter what others think of your path or choices, nor does it make any difference how long it takes you to learn the lesson. There is no wasted time or forsaken years — there is only the journey to become a better person.

As much as some may consider childhood a cliché, we are who we are for a reason. Just as the soil a seed is planted in makes all the difference in how it grows, the same is true for us. We are planted in an environment and family that our soul signed up for, not just to experience, but to grow from. The only way to do that is to heal what was hurt and allow ourselves to become the people we truly are when everything else is stripped away.

Ultimately, astrology helps show you who you are and what kind of life and relationship will be most in alignment with that. It also helps you understand that your truth is yours before you even realize it. Your truth may not be the popular choice, and likely it will take you away from certain situations and relationships, but looking for it is always a journey worth taking. Only in discovering your truth will you be able to love another from that authentic space. When you love from your inner truth, you are able not only to see yourself consciously but to be more present and accepting of your partner. You can talk about the difficult issues as they arise, advocate for your needs, and realize that love is so much more than just a passionate connection.

It's when your truth aligns with the truth of another, when both of you have removed your masks and you're standing free as sovereign beings under the light of the full moon ready to go all in, that love finally finds you. You are able to be by each other's side and to trust in the process of life, knowing it's not the journey to find each other that matters most, but what you make of the one you will take together. And when it comes to love, no one really wants to reach the destination anyway, because to create a forever love means that you will continue to grow together, to expand, and to realize that the magic really always does exist outside of your comfort zone.

The reason the journey to find your twin flame or healthy divine love is so profound is that you first have to complete the journey of finding yourself. Until you have made acquaintance with your authentic self, it's your conditioning, wounding, and fears that are determining the romantic choices you make. And while for most of this journey, you may not even realize you're not operating as your full self, once you meet your truth, everything changes within a moment. To know yourself is to know love. To understand who you are apart from the wounds means that you're in the position to make the decisions from your healing and your truth, which is what goes into the creation of a forever love. And as you do, you come to discover that the fullest embodiment of love is in fact truth.

It's Not Attachment — It's Love

In working with clients, it always seems to me that this third love is the one that can be the most challenging. Not only because you are engaging in the act of receiving, but because, as both of you continue to explore your individual journeys, you will have to grapple with a newfound freedom and autonomy. Recently, I spoke with Lucas, who had been in his first healthy relationship for about a year. Lucas had been through numerous lessons in his romantic journey and had to learn to be able to receive consistency and presence without seeking to use the presence of another to fill the holes left by his childhood wounds. Lucas told me that he knew his relationship with Mateo was different from any he'd been in before. Yet while he celebrated this fact, it was also causing him some doubts.

Lucas had only ever been in relationships in which he experienced a strong attachment to his partner. This attachment was the call to become aware of his childhood wounds; he had to remain in his karmic unions to process and learn the necessary lessons, after which he would need to figure out what love is without that same attachment. Lucas knew he loved Mateo, but that love didn't have the urgent life-or-death feeling that we often associate with the early relationship phase. Instead, he knew that he trusted Mateo, he knew that this was a relationship that was going to progress, and so he experienced a greater freedom than he was accustomed to.

The theory of attachment is based on the work of John Bowlby, a British psychoanalyst who focused on the relationships between children and their parents and identified four styles of attachment. This original theory has been expanded by other social scientists to include romantic relationships. While there are many variations of attachment styles, such as disorganized or ambivalent, in the journey of love, three become the most important: anxious, avoidant, and secure. What is interesting is that while the journey to create a relationship with your twin flame or divine healthy love requires your own growth and healing, it also takes you on a path to heal your attachment style, which is the direct result of your childhood.

Most people who grew up in a home where nothing was discussed, where everything was swept neatly under the rug, will develop an *avoidant attachment style*. That means they will ghost, stonewall, or otherwise avoid any sort of confrontation or emotionally intense conversation. Those who, on the other hand, were around arguing, experienced instability, or were made to feel overly responsible for others' well-being at a young age (a phenomenon called *parentification*) will develop a more *anxious attachment style*. These people need constant reassurance, communication, and explanations in order to find safety in a romantic relationship. In both the soulmate and the karmic union, the majority of people will exhibit either an avoidant or an anxious attachment style, as the healing of their inner child hasn't yet taken place.

Lucas was moving from the elusive dynamic of the anxious (his style) and avoidant (his previous partners') to a more secure attachment. For those who haven't experienced romantic love without an unhealthy attachment, which can feel a lot like love, a healthy relationship can feel completely foreign. As Lucas and I spoke, he began to understand that this new partner Lucas had attracted wasn't avoidant and did not trigger his anxious tendencies, and so his new partner was able to help support him in developing a more secure attachment. In these past relationships, he had also experienced the physical effects of his nervous system being triggered, which can show up as sweaty palms, an elevated heart rate, shaking, and the feeling of a looming crisis. But as he began to heal his inner child and to work with the affirmations "I am safe" and "I can keep myself safe," he shifted toward a more secure attachment, which he then brought into his relationship with Mateo.

Your attachment style is as much a part of your truth as how you define love. Until you become aware of how you tend to attach, you will continue to act unknowingly in your romantic choices. And as you become more secure, instead of seeking someone to provide the friction to grow, as Lucas had previously done, you will attract someone who is on a similar vibrational frequency as you. While Lucas and I were speaking about how to see the situation in his relationship as a green flag, we also talked about the importance of having some grace toward himself and that even while healing, he was still bound to become triggered.

In no relationship, including your third love, are you ever at the point where you are completely healed, perfect, or infallible, simply because you are a human and life is an ongoing journey. The growth that occurs before this union doesn't mean you'll never become triggered again, but you *will* react differently. For instance, instead of reacting from a place of anxious attachment, Lucas was able to practice positive self-talk and hold space to create a healthier outcome for himself and the relationship. It's about realizing what wounds are being triggered, understanding what you need, and learning to advocate for yourself to bring about compromise and healthy communication in your relationship.

The healthy divine love, a product of your own truth and healing, helps you approach your relationship from an ever-evolving best self. Instead of self-sabotaging or existing in the fight-or-flight state of a heightened nervous system, you can find the inner peace and acceptance necessary to work toward the resolution you and your partner need. Your truth can be challenging to discover if you're avoiding it or putting others ahead of yourself, which is why this journey has many layers. And it always ends up being about the person you grow into and then the love you create from there, rather than about any specific person.

Just as your fate is destined in the stars, so too is your healing. And as far as you've come on this journey, there is always more to be revealed. What's different now is that, rather than learning through pain or betrayal, as you did in the soulmate and karmic unions, you will be learning through love, just as Lucas has. To grow together with your twin flame or divine healthy love means to also keep growing yourself, to embrace your autonomy and honor your truth, and to recognize that never again will you have to sacrifice either in order to make a relationship work.

Your Soft Love Era

Divine love relationships are always continually evolving, but unlike previous relationships, you and your partner are doing it together. You may each change careers or take off on different international travels, but still your growth is taking place simultaneously. You never have to fear outgrowing your partner, because in this love, the more you grow, the closer you become.

Everything you have been through has prepared you for this love, and it doesn't matter whether you're twenty-seven or fifty-seven, this love exists for you. There is beauty in lessons, but there is a sweet reality in healing that nothing else can compare to. Here in this moment you are ready to finally allow love to be easy, to be soft. To recognize that a relationship isn't a battle that needs to be waged every day. It doesn't need to have claw marks where you are hanging on, and it doesn't ask that you play games in order to keep it going. Instead, it invites you to enter a realm of soft receiving, of allowing the connection to be comfortable and genuine, and to relax into the space of security, as you know this is the connection that you've been preparing for your whole life.

You've probably heard the term *soft girl era*; this is a connection that asks you to surrender into your *soft love era*. Instead of it being about self-care or rest for yourself, this love wraps you in the sensation of receiving what you've always longed for as you let it come rest gently in your soul. Your soft love era of the twin flame or healthy divine love is where you are both feeling secure, stable, and at ease within the connection. You have created a container of abundance for your relationship but still are each maintaining your own individual lives. Practicing compassion, accountability, and trust, you are able to show up as your best and ever-evolving selves the majority of the time. It's where you no longer need the push and pull of the avoidant and anxious, where the emotionally unavailable is no longer a lure. At this point you can see why you walked away from previous relationships that didn't resonate with your truth, because now you understand that when someone is truly ready for a romantic relationship mentally, emotionally, and physically, it will come with ease.

Your soft love era is one where you open to receive a love that genuinely does feel like home — even if it's a home you have never before known. You address issues as they arise, have healthy communication, and never worry that your partner will disappear or that it will all be taken away in a moment of ghosting. To enter into your soft love era means you also know that it's what you deserve. That you are worthy of love coming easily, even if it's between two imperfect, ever-healing adults. And because of this, it's the one that can last forever.

In your soft love era, you are ready to open your heart, to care for your inner child, to step into your healing adult self, and to embrace life for all that it's meant to be. And no matter how long it takes for you to do those things, it's all for a purpose, all for a reason. Because when you reach this point in your life, you are being divinely prepared to seize the next part of your journey, where it's not just about that amazing love but about living a life fully grounded in your unbridled truth.

Twin Flame and Divine Love Relationships
Charts and Journal Prompts

Fill in the blank charts below to create the birth charts for yourself, your partner, and your familial relationships. Or you can also download blank charts from my website at WordsOfKateRose.com.

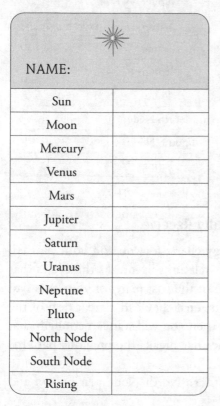

NAME:	
Sun	
Moon	
Mercury	
Venus	
Mars	
Jupiter	
Saturn	
Uranus	
Neptune	
Pluto	
North Node	
South Node	
Rising	

NAME:	
Sun	
Moon	
Mercury	
Venus	
Mars	
Jupiter	
Saturn	
Uranus	
Neptune	
Pluto	
North Node	
South Node	
Rising	

NAME:	
Sun	
Moon	
Mercury	
Venus	
Mars	
Jupiter	
Saturn	
Uranus	
Neptune	
Pluto	
North Node	
South Node	
Rising	

NAME:	
Sun	
Moon	
Mercury	
Venus	
Mars	
Jupiter	
Saturn	
Uranus	
Neptune	
Pluto	
North Node	
South Node	
Rising	

Open to Fully Receive

As you start to look at the astrology charts for you and your partner, it's important to focus on how this relationship breaks the cycles that have been in place. For example, if in the past many of your exes had the same rising sign as your parents, or if they had a great deal of the energy of one specific zodiac sign, then you will want to confirm that this current relationship is the one that breaks the previous patterns you have been moving through.

Reflect on your and your partner's North Node placements and how they align with each other or with other placements within your charts, as well as how the energy of your Venus works with your partner's. You are looking for understanding, a complementary love language, and how you both are guided to fulfill a similar purpose in your life.

This is the relationship that breaks all of the cycles of wounding, and so you may also see that your twin flame or divine love partner's chart lacks any similarities to those of your parents or caregivers. However, because this relationship is about giving you what you've always desired, you may find commonalities between their chart and the placements in the healthiest parental relationship that you experienced. This doesn't mean it's history repeating itself, but only that you had to move through the lessons that you did before you could fully receive the kind of love you've always desired.

The most important chart aspects with this relationship are that there won't be commonalities between your partner's chart and that of the familial relationship that felt lacking or contributed to your wounding. For example, there won't be a similar crossover with Saturn or the South Node. This will be the love that doesn't just break your previous patterns but also represents generational healing, as you are ushered into a new timeline and a new way of existing within a romantic relationship.

As you compare the charts and reflect on what makes up this relationship, consider asking yourself the following questions:

How is this relationship different from others you've had?
Does this relationship meet me in truth?
Are my partner and I at similar growth points on our journeys?
Is there a commonality in the future that we are called to create?
How does this relationship challenge my previous visions of love?

What have I had to heal in order to receive this love into my
life?

Does my current partner align with a positive familial relationship I had in childhood?

Do I feel as if this relationship serves a higher purpose for
myself and my partner?

Is the biggest challenge to fully receive this love into my life?
What are the obstacles preventing me from doing this,
and do I need to release or heal anything to accomplish it?

Have I allowed myself to surrender into my soft era and let
love to be easy?

Am I remaining dedicated to my own journey and accom-
plishments, even in connection?

While your other relationships taught you lessons through lack
or pain, this is the union that will be able to help you expand by fully
receiving love. It likely will progress more quickly than you expected,
because once each person has identified their own truth and is operating as their healing adult self, romantic decisions suddenly become
much easier.

No longer do you need years or even decades to figure out if someone is truly meant to be in your life and is aligned with your healing.
You're ready to let this relationship progress however it naturally does,
even if your logical self thinks it's happening too fast, as this union
will continually feel right no matter the speed at which it moves.
Allow yourself to surrender to this love, to fully accept that this is the
cycle-breaker relationship, and to receive all of the love you've ever
desired.

You were born worthy, and now you are able to open to receive
that deliciously ripe love you've spent a lifetime dreaming about.

Affirmations for the Twin Flame
and Divine Love Relationship

I am safe.

I am worthy of receiving all that I have ever desired from love.

I deserve a safe, passionate, and consistent love.

I am practicing grace for myself.

I no longer need to be perfect; I only need to be myself.

This love is not like the ones that came before.

I will pause when I feel triggered and lean into my inner self before reacting.

I am able to communicate my needs, wants, and desires safely and with ease.

I no longer need love to be a struggle but can accept its ease.

I am able to create security within myself that is mirrored in my romantic relationship with my partner.

I am free to create the life and love of my dreams.

I am honoring my inner truth with each decision that I make.

I am worthy to be fully seen and loved for who I am.

I am safe to open my heart, to be vulnerable, and to trust that my partner has my best interests at heart.

I am ready for a love that will last forever.

I am committed to becoming my best self, and I forgive myself when I can't be.

Moon Rituals for the Twin Flame and Divine Love Relationship

Moon rituals are powerful moments to reflect on all that has been and to focus your energy on what you want to invite into your life. While the soulmate and karmic relationships were more about release, in the twin flame rituals, it's about setting an intention for growing a continued bond with another. Yet at different points on the journey you may also need to release fears, doubts, or even old beliefs that you hadn't realized were still taking up space in your psyche.

These moon rituals ask you to remember that this divine love is one that will continually move you into deeper self-healing as you expand to receive all you have ever desired and deserved. Sometimes the scariest thing in the world isn't being in the karmic relationship but finally having what you've always dreamed of. Practicing compassion for yourself is what will allow you to move forward as you release what you've outgrown so you can grow into the new and softer era of your life.

Full Moon Self-Healing Ritual

Lean into all that you have become on this journey and embrace a continual process of self-healing as you honor your own cycle and the synchronicity of the moon. Recognize that in this ritual it's about releasing, not a relationship, but anything within you that no longer resonates with your truth. Your twin flame isn't a love whose sole purpose is to impart a lesson, but one that represents the cumulation of a lifetime of healing and growth. Yet even reaching that stage doesn't mean you are now perfect; you are called to hold the parts of yourself that may still be in survival mode and to remind yourself that you are safe to release what you no longer need to protect you.

You are now in the transition from allowing fear to keep you safe to instead allowing love to keep you safe. As you lower the walls around your heart, think about what you can let go of to make more space for love to grow. Whether it's old fears, wounds from your karmic relationship, or trepidation about being vulnerable with someone again, you are releasing what is necessary to create the space to receive this love more fully into your heart and life. Reflect, too, on whether you have decided to try to maintain a friendship or acquaintance with your karmic partner, as you may be called to release that. Even if you have to coparent with them, you may find you need better boundaries in order to move forward into the love you desire.

Let yourself soften, breathe deeply, and know that you are safe — safe to love and safe to release all that no longer resonates with your truth and healing.

Healing Crystals

Amazonite: This crystal helps to build your self-esteem as you honor what you are worthy of receiving. It will enhance your ability to feel empowered and to focus your energy on your overall well-being.

Iolite: This is an important stone because it helps you heighten your beliefs about what living an amazing life and having an amazing love represent. You can use iolite to gain clarity, communicate with ease, and embody all that you deserve from your relationship.

Red Jasper: Allow yourself to ground into what is real, to feel protected and nurtured in this new part of your life, as you imbibe the healing powers of this stone. Along with an increase in passion and abundance, red jasper lets you embrace what is being offered to you and to trust that it's real.

How to Perform the Full-Moon Ritual of Self-Healing

Full moons are a time for release, but in this situation, you aren't trying to cut the energetic cords of a past relationship; instead, you are doing some inner emotional housekeeping. To prepare for the ritual, take some time to reflect on what you need to release or heal in order to create more space for love. Then write down on a piece of paper, "I am releasing..." followed by the beliefs or fears you no longer need.

This ritual would best be done on the full moon in your moon sign or in the opposite sign. For instance, if you are an Aquarius moon, then you can do it on the full moon in Aquarius or its opposite sign, Leo. If you feel called to do this ritual soon and there's a significant amount of time before you can do it in your moon sign or the opposing sign, then feel free to do it under whatever full moon you wish, as that celestial body will still hold the power necessary to help you create space for your healthy love.

Begin by finding a space outside, preferably in your garden, and then dig a small hole in the earth.

Place a white candle inside the hole (a tea light will work too). Arrange a wreath around the candle using cuttings from eucalyptus and sage and some marigold petals, which will bring in joy.

When you're ready, find a comfortable place to sit on the ground, your body connected with the earth, and then light your candle.

Read your letter aloud about what you are releasing, followed by the affirmations "I am free. I am healing. I am creating space for love." Repeat the affirmations of your choosing while you safely burn your letter and then scatter the ashes around the candle.

Once the candle has burned out, cover the ritual materials with earth and place a stone on top. Or, if you don't have one, sprinkle a bit of sage and moon water over the burial site to close out that chapter of your life. (To make moon water, leave a glass of water outside where it can be infused with the energy of moonlight. Although it's most powerful at full moons, you can create moon water during any lunar phase.)

After you're finished, draw a bath or shower, and as you are cleansing your body, repeat the affirmation "I am washing off the old to make space for the new." Massage a heart-opening salve with jasmine or rose into your skin. Then, allow yourself to rest and savor what it feels like in your body to surrender into your soft love era.

New Moon Manifestation Ritual

A new moon is a time to set an intention for what you want to attract or grow in your life. It's a moment when you are planting the seeds for what you want to reap. Whether you are already in connection with your divine healthy love or you want to attract it into your life, you can use this ritual to set an intention for what you know you deserve.

If you are single and know you are looking to call in your divine love partner, then perform the ritual during your opposing moon sign for the most power. For example, if you are a Piscean moon, then it's best to work with the energy of the Virgo new moon, the opposite of Pisces. If that seems too far off, then do the ritual during a new moon in an earth sign, which is perfect for growing something new, or during any new moon that resonates deeply with you.

Even if you have discovered that you are in your twin flame or divine love relationship already, you can still set an intention for new growth in your connection. This isn't to call in a new relationship but, rather, to honor the one you've already built while you commit to deepening the connection or focus on the future that you want to create together.

The most important thing to remember about this new moon manifestation ritual is that you are calling something unique and new into your life. You are embracing life as a healing adult and setting an intention to create or nurture a profound and healthy romantic connection. This is the moment when you have found freedom from what you were and now the only thing left to do is simply open to fully receive the romantic relationship of your dreams.

Healing Crystals

Blue Aragonite: This crystal helps you continue to advocate for your truth. It activates your throat chakra, the seat of your voice, and can teach you to communicate in a healthy and profound way as you seek to build a romantic connection based on honesty, transparency, and love.

Strawberry Quartz: Allow yourself to embrace your passionate and sexual nature as you create a sacred bond with your romantic partner. This quartz helps to attract positive energy, joy, and abundance into this new chapter of your life.

Unakite: Regardless of your personal beliefs, this stone helps to create a bridge to the spiritual world. Allow yourself to find inner balance and then transfer that into your relationship, if you are in one. Let yourself believe that this union truly was written in the stars and surrender to the deep and powerful transformation it brings to your life.

How to Perform the New Moon Ritual of Manifestation

You have reached a place where you can set an intention for what you want to attract into your life because you know who you truly are. You understand what you need from a partner, not in a superficial way, but in a way that will resonate with your authentic soul. You validate your desires and know that you are truly worthy of receiving all that you long for from life and love.

To begin, light a pink candle and write down what you are calling into your life, being as specific as possible. If you already are in your third love relationship, then you can add your and your partner's names as well. Reflect on what kind of relationship you want, how you want to be loved, or how you envision setting up your life together.

Once you're finished, fold the paper three times toward you to manifest this intention into your life. Then, draw a heart on the paper and write your name and the words "Divine Love" or "Twin Flame" on it. Or, if you are in a relationship, write down your and your partner's names. Then, drip melted pink wax from the candle over the paper until it covers the heart fully. You can do this over a piece of wax paper or outside on the earth.

After you've covered the heart in pink wax, you are going to use the paper to make an intention bundle. Take a square of violet or white fabric about the size of a cloth napkin, lay it out flat, and place your paper with the intention inside, along with rose petals for love, verbena or lemon peels for truth, and pomegranate seeds for passion.

Repeat an affirmation that resonates for you, such as "I am fully receiving a soft love," "I am attracting a healthy love," or "I am setting an intention to deepen my soft love," as you bind the fabric up with white ribbon.

Plant your intention bundle beneath a rosebush or place it on your altar.

As you finish your ritual, you can brew a mug of basil and rose tea, adding orange-infused honey, to enjoy by yourself or with your partner.

Continue to receive and surrender into your healthy, amazing love, trusting that this time it truly is different.

Conclusion
Letting the Stars Lead the Way

Just as the universe has always had your back, the stars have always led your way.

To understand what was written in the stars for you is to also understand yourself. This knowledge helps you practice compassion and grace toward yourself as you navigate the flurry of life lessons and moments of heartbreak, because you know a higher purpose is always at play.

The moments when you almost gave up hope for love were the very ones that were guiding you to go deep within, to see that it's not that you got it all wrong, but that you were in the process of learning how to get it right.

There are no mistakes on your journey of love; there is no wasted time. Everything is happening precisely as it's meant to. As you move through your lessons, you will also learn why things had to happen in the way that they did.

To let the stars lead the way is to be open to accepting the larger purpose that is at play in your life. It is an encouragement to never give up hope that your lifetime forever love is still out there.

Both life and love tend to take a path of unexpectedness, as things seldom go according to plan. You are left to embrace flexibility and to discover the greater meaning of events. You will also realize that your relationship is not ultimately about sex, company, or having a family together. Its purpose is to guide you back toward yourself. That is where the stars are leading you.

When you can understand that each relationship, each decision was a reflection of where you were with yourself at the time, then you can also see what it is that you need to give yourself. This will always be the key to creating a relationship that fulfills your soul in ways you've only dreamed of.

But you have to be okay with having some love that is meant to last only for a moment and not a lifetime.

You have to accept that to achieve what you've always desired, you will need to make the very changes you never wanted to make, and you will go through experiences that will bring you to your knees.

Because only on your knees can you surrender to the universe.

As much as your heart may have hurt in the past or perhaps is breaking as you read this, it is all occurring so that you can become better, because ultimately that is the purpose of love.

Your relationship, whether it lasts for a decade or a lifetime, will challenge you to evolve into your fully healing adult self. Only then are you able to receive the love you have always desired in your life.

Understand that while no one chooses to go on this journey, it is already at play in the very first instances of butterflies and attraction, because each moment, each encounter, is destined in the stars.

To let the stars lead the way means to have faith, to trust, and to never again let yourself hang onto someone because you fear what may happen if you don't. It gives you the willingness to surrender to the process of becoming, not knowing who you will transform into or where it will all lead.

There is never a moment that the universe isn't supporting you and isn't behind each and every event in your life. Everything is always happening for your highest good.

Accept that things went differently than you had imagined they would, receive the lessons that love has brought to your doorstep, and then sit with your heart in a place of peace as you fully focus on yourself.

Your great love is out there.

It may not come as you expected, and you may have to face parts of yourself and your past that you never planned to, but through it all, your person is out there doing the same.

While you were moving through the spaces of learning and blundered confusion, your person was as well. As the stars have been leading you, they've also been directing the path of the one who is meant to love you for a lifetime.

Nothing is lost, and nothing is wasted, because as you surrender into the arms of love, time evaporates in the fulfillment of understanding.

To love, you first have to be broken open.

To receive what you've always desired, you have to heal the feelings of lack.

And to move into your soft love era, you also must release love that is a struggle.

Because you have always been destined for more.

You have always deserved to be loved for precisely who you are, and now that you've learned what that means, you will be.

All it takes is a moment to change everything, and as the universe reveals the truth that was written in the stars, you can finally exhale, knowing all you desire may be just around the next corner of change.

The best truly is yet to come, and now you are finally in the place not just to receive it — but to live it.

Keep loving and letting the stars lead the way,
Kate xx

Acknowledgments

After my first book, *You Only Fall in Love Three Times: The Secret Search for Our Twin Flame*, the number one question I received was, "But how do you know which relationship you are in?" Because of that, and because appearances can be deceiving but love is always truthful, I began my own quest to provide understanding and confirmation to all those who asked. Without that question, *Written in the Stars* might never have come to fruition, so thank you to everyone who reached out and spurred the journey to begin writing this book. The subsequent research behind identifying astrological patterns for the soulmate, karmic, and twin flame relationships wouldn't have been possible without readers and clients being willing to share their lives and birth information with me, so for that, too, I express deep gratitude and thanks.

As always, I am grateful to my agent, Joseph Durepos, who has continually believed in my projects, even if, in his words, he didn't quite understand astrology. And thank you, Jason Gardner, Kristen Cashman, and Diana Rico with New World Library, for taking on this project and contributing as much heart to bring it to life as I did in writing it.

Thank you to my incredible daughters, who understand what it means to have a writer as a mother. I am eternally grateful for your patience, flexibility, support, and love.

And for you, the reader who decided you were ready for the truth and purchased *Written in the Stars*, I hope this will help you on your journey of love, so that you can find gratitude not just for where it leads, but for all you experienced along the way.

Quick-Reference Guide to Key Terms and Concepts

Meanings of the Planets in Genealogical Astrology

Sun: The sun in astrology governs your external self, or how you appear to others, though it's not necessarily representative of your true nature. The way you present as a result of your sun sign can determine who you are attracted to and who is attracted to you, but this initial attraction often doesn't lead to a deeper connection that can sustain and grow a relationship long-term.

Moon: The moon governs your emotional body. While all the planets go into creating your authentic self, the moon often is considered the truest part of yourself. Your moon sign affects not only your emotional feelings but also what is most important to you and how you see the world.

Mercury: Mercury is the planet that rules communication. In genealogical astrology it represents how you communicate, how you need to be spoken to, and what will be most important for you to discuss in relationships.

Venus: Venus is the planet of love, and while it's no surprise that this planet is of importance to your romantic connections, its significance goes beyond that. Not only does Venus affect how you love and need to be loved by your partner, but it also represents the love you needed as a child, making this a particularly crucial planet for identifying the wounds of your childhood in your astrology chart.

Mars: Mars governs passion and intimacy; it also affects your motivation and determination. Because Mars rules over masculine energy, you can often see Mars patterns emerge in your genealogical astrology charts, patterns that point to what is important to you and to any wounds you are in the process of healing.

Jupiter: Jupiter is the planet of luck and abundance; it also represents the future or the far-off horizon of your dreams. Jupiter can be especially important in helping you attract someone on the basis of the kind of life you perceive you will create together. Jupiter can also be significant in bringing you together with a romantic partner who can help you build the type of life that you wish you'd had in childhood. Its power isn't only that of luck but of healing as well.

Saturn: Saturn is the planet of divine timing and karmic lessons, but in this type of astrology it actually governs your soulmate relationship. Saturn seeks to teach you how to be more yourself by attracting someone who is a reflection of where you are at the time of meeting. Saturn rules over your personal karmic lessons versus those that are generational or derived from childhood wounding.

Uranus, Neptune, and Pluto: While these three planets represent a significant dynamic in your own life experiences, in genealogical astrology, they adhere to their meaning of *generational planets*. Generational planets are named as such because they change signs so infrequently, every seven to twenty years. When you see similarities between your Uranus, Neptune, and/or Pluto placements and those of your partner, it simply means you are part of the same generation.

North Node: The North Node governs your fate, the ultimate representation of your soul contract and what you were born into this life to fulfill. But to be able to choose to follow your destiny, you first must learn the lessons associated with your South Node.

South Node: The South Node is known as the place of the soul's undoing, as it represents your generational and childhood karma. The South Node will frequently show up with importance in your karmic relationships, as this connection will produce a turning point in your own growth and move you closer to the love you have always dreamed of.

Rising sign: Also known as the ascending or ascendant sign, your rising sign serves as an umbrella under which your entire birth chart resides. This is a leading energy that is just as dominant as your sun sign or North Node. It can help you understand yourself and your partner more deeply.

Identifying the Elements of Each Zodiac Sign

If your birth chart doesn't list the leading elements, you can discover them for yourself by counting up the number of each earth, air, fire, and water zodiac signs that are present.

Earth: Taurus, Virgo, and Capricorn
Air: Aquarius, Gemini, and Libra
Fire: Aries, Leo, and Sagittarius
Water: Cancer, Scorpio, and Pisces

Masculine and Feminine Energies

While many birth charts will list masculine and feminine (or *aggressive and passive*, as they are sometimes known) placements, you can also refer to this list to count up the number of each that you personally possess:

Masculine Zodiac Signs: Aries, Gemini, Leo, Libra, Sagittarius, and Aquarius

Feminine Zodiac Signs: Taurus, Cancer, Virgo, Scorpio, Capricorn, and Pisces

About the Author

Kate Rose is a therapist, relationship expert, and international bespoke retreat curator. She is also a popular online writer whose articles have reached more than 75 million people in 275 countries in a little over six years. As a spiritual intuitive and astrologer, she uses the stars to clarify our purpose and help us see the as-yet-unlearned lessons that are blocking us from the life we are destined to live. Her first book, *You Only Fall in Love Three Times*, has been published in eleven different countries and continues to change the landscape of love and relationships. Through her writings and therapy practice, she has become one of the leading voices in the world on soulmate, karmic, and twin flame relationships. She has pioneered the ever-growing awareness around conscious relationships as well as the connection between the healing of self and finding our forever love. Kate lives surrounded by love in the Hidden Hills of Massachusetts, where she can embrace the natural beauty of the area to find peace. She has been a passionate yogi for over a decade and looks forward to practicing yin yoga and yoga nidra every week, in between making the most of each day with her two incredible daughters. Kate has a soft spot for her fluffy kitty boys and for cooking to music while she dances around her kitchen. For her, every day is a practice of leading with love. For more, see WordsOfKateRose.com.

NEW WORLD LIBRARY is dedicated to publishing books and other media that inspire and challenge us to improve the quality of our lives and the world.

We are a socially and environmentally aware company. We recognize that we have an ethical responsibility to our readers, our authors, our staff members, and our planet.

We serve our readers by creating the finest publications possible on personal growth, creativity, spirituality, wellness, and other areas of emerging importance. We serve our authors by working with them to produce and promote quality books that reach a wide audience. We serve New World Library employees with generous benefits, significant profit sharing, and constant encouragement to pursue their most expansive dreams.

We print our books with soy-based ink on paper from sustainably managed forests. We power our Northern California office with solar energy, and we respectfully acknowledge that it is located on the ancestral lands of the Coast Miwok Indians. We also contribute to nonprofit organizations working to make the world a better place for us all.

Our products are available wherever books are sold.

customerservice@NewWorldLibrary.com
Phone: 415-884-2100 or 800-972-6657
Orders: Ext. 110
Fax: 415-884-2199
NewWorldLibrary.com

Scan below to access our newsletter
and learn more about our books and authors.